ALL WILL BE WELL

"Michael Meegan is quite simply inspirational. It is
an extraordinary experience to encounter someone so
living in the present."
The Irish Times

"Full of delight and joy, gentleness, honour and grace."
Sunday Tribune

"Powerful, disturbing and beautiful."
John Hurt

ALL WILL BE WELL

Michael Meegan

Edited by Julie Pearson

Published by Eye Books

All Will Be Well
2nd Edition
August 2004

Published by Eye Books Ltd
51a Boscombe Rd
London
W12 9HT
Tel/fax: +44 (0) 20 8743 3276
website: www.eye-books.com

Set in Frutiger and Garamond
ISBN: 1903070279

British Library Cataloguing in Publication Data
A catalogue record for this book is available from the British Library

Printed and bound in Great Britain by Biddles Ltd

This book is dedicated to Joe who has always lived his dreams, sung a different song and danced with children. Joe always believes in the impossible.

He taught me that you can always think outside the box if you have no box. When I grow up I'd like to be like Joe and always remember what matters.

To my dear and beloved physician and
fellow pilgrim, Dr Joe Barnes.

All royalties from this book will go to child survival, women's health and AIDS programmes in Africa.

Acknowledgements

True friends are not those who come to your parties and celebrations, they are the ones who help you clear up the mess afterwards. The friends you have with you all your life are those who come to you when the rest of the World has just walked out on you. My heart goes to those who have accepted me in all my fragility and weakness, accepted me despite knowing the whole of me. These friends I am delighted to say are so woven into my world that they know from my eyes who they are, and from my kiss.

My wisest companion, Ronan Conroy has shared many adventures. Ronan has taught me so much about learning and growing, and for his infinite patience and insight, gracias. To the whole team at Eye Books who have become good friends and especially Julie Pearson and Jennifer Glass for all their help in editing this book, asante. Dr Tom O'Riordan walked at my side from the very beginning of my own journey and has been there ever since, a childhood friend whose heart is deep and spirit old, he believed when there was no reason to, ashe. In Africa I live and work with the most wonderful companions none of whom see anything we do as a job. For their laughter, magic and joy, pamoja! Bean and John always welcome me to their home in Ireland, there are few things more defining than sharing your home, having a place to feel welcome, for that I have no words.

And then there's you my friends, sharing these reflections. We are if only for a few hours together and you are taking time to hear what I have to share. This too is a communion, this is a looking at the stars, wondering, discovering... and I will leave it to one greater than I to thank you.

CONTENTS

1 THE JOURNEY 1

2 THE SEARCH FOR MEANING 19

3 THE DANCE 53

4 SECRETS OF JOY 91

5 BECOMING 105

EPILOGUE: THE FOOTBALL LESSON 137

THE JOURNEY

'It is only with the heart that one sees clearly,
what is essential is invisible to the eye.'

The Little Prince

We were not designed to live the lifestyle that has become predominant today. The nature of our Western economy is to feed an insatiable value system based on having more. It is based on people not being happy. If people began thinking that they were content with what they possessed already, the economy could no longer sell you the latest style or the latest 'must-have' stuff. We live in a time of self-preoccupation and a culture of self-absorption. We settle for trifles such as wealth, fame and comfort but human beings are more complex than that, which is why there is such an industry built around seeking – lifestyle changes, nutrition, 'getting your life back', staying young, having a better sex life, how to be more confident. Such self-help books, at their best, can do three things. They can remind people that they are locked into cycles and patterns of negative thinking; they can point out practical ways of changing behaviour or developing self-awareness and they can help people to climb out of emotional straitjackets: but these are merely by-products of a way of life that we were never meant to live in the first place.

The fact that self-help literature has been the fastest growing sector of popular books over the last decade indicates there is a real need but we should not allow ourselves to surrender the formation of our own ideas and opinions to others.

It is often easier to read about happiness than to become happy, easier to aspire than to do, easier to plan than to break the entrenched patterns of our daily routine. We are actually being told what we already know – that to be whole, we need to recognise our complete selves, to accept and love ourselves. To grow, we need to know where we are and in order to enjoy life, we need to let go. This cannot be achieved through books offering quick fixes or instant solutions such as '60 second stress relief' or 'How to become happy in 5 minutes.'

The things we want to come home to at night, the things that make us cry with joy, the things that fill us with utter delight – these are things we cannot buy or rationalise.

All life is about relationships. All human relationships are about light and dark, positive energy and draining energy. They are a dynamic flow of life force. Our interactions are closely linked to that vibe, that karma or chemistry that either draws us towards each other or keeps us apart. At an unconscious level, our instincts tell us a lot about those around us. More importantly, they also tell us about what is within us. The problem is, we do not always listen to our innate wisdom but instead to our reasoning.

I have deliberately departed from putting experiences into boxes because it is not the way we *really* think. I also doubt that thinking in straight lines is helpful. We have been taught to think logically, to reason and deduce. Scientific analysis too depends on rigid thought processes and rational models. But life is rarely logical or rational, and human experience stretches boundlessly beyond the constraints of the mind.

We all have basic needs. We all cry when we are hurt or rejected. We all bleed when we are beaten and we all thirst for love above all else. If we look, we find that most of the wonderful moments of our lives, the most magical moments, happen unplanned. They usually surprise us and they are usually very simple. The things we want to come home to at night, the things that make us cry with joy, the things that fill us with utter delight – these are things we cannot buy or rationalise.

In sharing my thoughts I do so without regard to time and place because what matters is not the minutiae but the big picture. Like all essential things, it is completely obvious and so clear that we can easily overlook it unless we think without our logical, adult heads.

I studied philosophy and theology, then science and languages but for myself, I have always found that thinking like a child is much more useful. I believe that the way in which people learn in school is damaging to the way in which our minds should be able to create and evolve. The concept of placing ideas into subjects and information into linear models binds thought processes, often burying children's imaginations. Our kids are growing up in front of TVs and computer screens having their possibilities ever reduced to the dimensions of Microsoft and cyberspace. But cyberspace is very small. The billions of three-dimensional gigabytes that shoot across the information superhighway are just that – more bits of other people's information. Children are, increasingly, not exploring the infinite possibilities of their own creative powers. They are not learning the many arts of sharing, communicating or expressing what is in their hearts.

Children, by nature, are insatiably curious, do not have rules or boundaries, do not fence in the range of possibilities, cannot see why not. Their sense of danger is overwhelmed by their sense of wonder. I would ask you to taste these thoughts with that same innocence. I have not written as a doctor or as a philosopher, or as an author. I am writing as a friend, as a child, as a fellow traveller. I look at the world

Everything is possibility. Everyone we meet is an opportunity. Every morning is full of chances to become, to change, to grow.

with unending curiosity and excitement. There is so much to delight in, so much to discover and awaken to. Everything is possibility. Everyone we meet is an opportunity. Every morning is full of chances to become, to change, to grow.

There are two journeys we make through life – the physical journey of the body, through time and space, and the internal voyage of the heart and soul that is somehow more challenging. There are moments in all our lives when we are deeply touched, inspired or enriched. There are also moments of anguish and pain, times of stress and confusion.

The way we are treated, profoundly affects the way we respond to others. Every one of us goes through life hoping to love and be loved. Much of our lives are spent trying to find a sense of belonging. Whatever the pursuit, whether it be to make money, possess things, be popular, have power; it is done in the belief that eventually we shall be happy but so often we get lost along the way. We can learn from each other, learn from how we are treated and in time, we can develop a map for our journey. In sharing our experiences we can become stronger, more aware, sometimes wiser. We

There were people alive who had never known what it was like to sleep in a warm bed, or eat a full meal, or have one good day.

cannot think of ourselves in isolation for we are all of us travellers on an uncertain journey; one of possibilities and choices where the decisions we make can change the energy, fabric and dynamics of our lives. The journey begins with the recognition that there is the same extraordinary energy within all of us, the same mystery, the same fire.

Who I am is not important but what I want to share is, I think, of real significance. I offer my thoughts as a fellow pilgrim. I share them with delight – please take what you like from them.

My own journey began with a realisation that seems self evident to me. My logic was crude and my reasoning child-like, but I trusted my instincts. For years on TV news I had seen images of people who were hurt. There were famines and wars and droughts. There were hungry kids, tragedy and pain. Like most young guys, I would change the channel over or become distracted by the next commercial. I had a busy social life and distant stories were just that, distant. They were not part of my world.

Growing up, I had never wanted for anything, I had a happy childhood, travelled a lot, and developed friendships that have lasted over thirty years. I was having a great life and was deeply content. The only jarring note came with an observation that there were human beings on our tiny globe who were really having a lousy time here. It was as simple as that. There were people alive who had never known what it was like to sleep in a warm bed, or eat a full meal, or have one good day. There were people who were simply trying to survive from one hour to the next. To my mind that was just bad.

I never doubted for a moment that I could do something.

I never thought for a single second that there was anything wrong with my lifestyle. I still liked nice restaurants, going to the cinema, music, girls, cycling holidays, hanging out with friends. For me, wanting to try and balance an obvious wrong did not mean I would be doing anything noble or charitable or acting out of a sense of guilt. There is something dangerous about calling basic justice charity and something unhealthy about exhibiting what we do for others.

I was aware that there were a lot of people in need at home. There were street kids, lonely old people, children in hospital, and so many ways in which to do so much. But I kept comparing my own fantastic life and the people who would never even dream about such a life. It was the opposite of guilt. It was a very simple but strong feeling that everyone should be able to enjoy the pleasures and freedoms I had. I never doubted for a moment that I could do something. If someone somewhere did not have anything, I could actually go and give them something. There really was nothing more to it, it was merely a question of getting off my backside. I had no intention of changing who I was. I wasn't on a mission, and I had no interest in sharing my idea with anyone.

I decided to express my gut feeling in Africa. It could have been in countless other ways; in countless other places in the world – the journey would have been essentially the same. The unfolding of a life; different places, different people but hopefully the same mystery, the same spark.

I had the idea of going to the Karamoja desert and doing something about the famine there. It was as simple an idea as that. That was many years ago, before the aid game became big business, before *The Lords of Poverty* was published. It

I was walking in the dark, but at least I was walking.

was a devastating expose of the misery industry and the manipulation of the poor by the World Bank, UN and other agencies whose extravagant misuse of resources created more poverty. It was long before Live Aid. I wanted to do something, but I was not quite sure what. I was walking in the dark, but at least I was walking.

Before I went to Africa, I read many books about malnutrition and starvation and what people could do about it. David Morley was the first professor of tropical child health and one of the most influential promoters of childhood development, his books, writings and insights changed the face of international health and continue to inspire health care

He taught me that unlearning what we know is as important as knowing how little we do know and the limits of what we know.

throughout the poor world. I had only ever heard of Professor Morley in this professional context until I finally got to meet the man. I had expected an oracle, an expert consultant type, a man who would give me five minutes and move on. I had already met a lot of people who made me feel stupid and plenty who told me not to even bother going to Africa. David Morley was not in his office as he had filled it with students who were short of space. He was somewhere beneath piles of work and experiments.

9

The first thing he did was to put a cup of tea in my hand and talk about what made children smile and why adults did not. He had the excitement of a small child and rooted through boxes showing me things. We knelt down to explore an invention, listened to children singing and he showed me ways children play. His passion blinded him to my ignorance and his excitement in everything was contagious. David was so receptive to all ideas, and almost 25 years later, we are still working together. After a lifetime of moving the boundaries of international health, David remains one of the most loved and respected child doctors in the world. His legacy is seen in health policies in most developing countries, and his openness and energy have inspired generations. David taught me that unlearning what we know is as important as knowing how little we do know and the limits of what we know. And so began in my mind the idea that I might *really* be able to do something. I believed then, and even more now, that there is a harmony in creation and that despite the failures in humanity everything will be well.

When we hear of so much human misery, it is far less painful for us to close the door than to allow the tide of suffering to overwhelm us.

Since then, so much has happened. The world we live in today is a very different place. The gap between the rich and poor is far greater now than we could ever have imagined.

The six richest people in the world own more than the six hundred million poorest.

If that doesn't surprise you, how about the three hundred richest people in the world owning more of the worlds wealth than half of humanity.

There are over eight hundred million people living in the world who are hungry.

We live in a world at war, a world polarising and dividing. Our society is troubled with depression and stress – the fastest growing health problems in the Western world. There seems to be a tidal wave of bad news every day: corruption, conflict, AIDS, violence, injustice, pain, suffering, sorrow... Lets face it, it's hard enough trying to survive the trauma of daily life without beginning to look too hard at the mess going on all around us. When we hear of so much human misery, it is far less painful for us to close the door than to allow the tide of suffering to overwhelm us.

In my life, the greatest inspiration has come from people.

Much of what is shared in this book cannot be explained away. There is no wonder in pointless suffering and poverty. I have no answers to these problems. I can only tell you what I am doing about it and the attitude with which I engage it. I do not get used to the pain and cruelty I see, but I believe it is more productive to channel my energy into action, than to give in to frustration or apathy.

I would like to share with you some of the beauty that has touched my life in the hope that it will enrich you in some way. I have always been amazed by the power of nature and the majesty of the universe. There are many things that can stun us into silence and awaken our senses. We can be lifted from ourselves by music and awoken by books that reach our inner-selves.

In my life, the greatest inspiration has come from people. You know the ones I mean, those whose passion and energy have no words. They are like children in that they see the simplicity and honesty of life. The people that touch us are rarely perfect, but they are awake. They are not icons but they aspire to be themselves. They rejoice in life, delight in being and make us feel better just through their presence. Such people cannot begin to comprehend cynicism or scepticism because their mind-sets see possibilities and opportunities, not doubts and dangers.

My journey is not about the distant lands to which I have travelled, the ancient tribes I have met, the awesome things I have seen, it is about wonder, it is about joy. At its heart are the lessons I have learnt from my experiences with the people who have danced into my life – some that have touched me and moved me to action, others that have enthralled me, still others who have set me on fire. Each of these are human and full of frailty which is why they are so important – they are like us.

The thoughts I will share with you have helped me enjoy my life and discover ways in which I could celebrate life in others. My hope is that these things are as familiar to your heart as your own memory and that by speaking of them they will remind you of something essential to who we are. I am going to tell you something of my own life, and the easiest way to do that is to do as my Irish forefathers did, *Religion has so often failed people with its platitudes.* and tell you stories. We can't always control the small print of our lives; our location, occupation or circumstance, but we can become the co-authors of our own journey. We can help write the story itself. The stories themselves are not really very important, it is the thread that runs through them that matters. Sometimes things can be transmitted from person to person in stories that just cannot be explained.

I went to Africa over twenty years ago. I went because I wanted to live among the poor and help them. I spent a long time in the homes of nomads in the Northern and Southern borders of Kenya, finally having my own manyattas and cow dung huts in the remote hills south of lake Turkana in the heart of the lands of the Samburu, and on the vast plains that stretch from the Serengeti across the Rift valley to the Ngong Hills.

Perhaps the greatest reason for the decline of spiritual awareness in the Western world has been religion.

In traditional rural Africa people think very differently about time and space and their relationship with nature. They also have a radically different concept of purpose, identity and achievement. Some of those foundations can perhaps enrich our own way of seeing what is going on around us and within us.

In my own becoming I learnt the languages of dreams, was able to play with children and talk long into the night with old men of legends and myths. I spoke in dialects that have almost vanished. I found that the things we remember about other people are rarely what they say. We recall their energy, their essence, their smell, the taste they leave, their eyes, their expressions and their tone.

While I hope that in your life your eyes do not see the pain and suffering I have seen, nor your ears hear the sorrow and sadness I have heard, nevertheless I share something of it in the hope that a moment of it touches some common part of us. Although coloured by my recollection and stained by my subjectivity, I believe there remains enough of the primordial current of those I remember to light a candle within you. What I share is of course only a pale reflection of what can never be known through words. I have a profound doubt about those who can preach some creed or belief. Certitude disturbs the deepest part of me.

Perhaps the greatest reason for the decline of spiritual awareness in the Western world has been religion. The packaging of God, of spirit, within denominations and the 'holier than thou' assumptions of the 'saved' has done what the devil couldn't; eroded the Church from within, not by argument but through complacency. People today are not looking for doctrine and dogma, ritual and liturgy – we are searching for meaning.

All around us there are opportunities to care, chances to comfort, potential to build, possibilities to love.

So when I talk about the sacred, I am not talking about religion or belief or even a particular set of principals. There are no boxes. Being real to yourself, to me, suggests three things, 'Is not religion all deeds and all reflection? Who can separate his faith from his actions, or his belief from his occupation? The anger or fear we sometimes feel when religion is mentioned stems from a revulsion to the hypocrisy and corruption that has been seen in institutional churches over the ages. The church men, the scandals, the gross abuses and ambition, the failures, have soured many people to the most innocent reference to anything that might imply the holy. This has a lot to do with the current perception that the spirit is somehow the reserve religion.

With love, there are no rules

We often define religion too narrowly. It is not a membership but an understanding of what life is about. There are signs that more and more people are seeking a personal relationship, without the intermediation of an institution telling them what God is supposed to be. Religion has so often failed people with its platitudes. When it comes to questions of meaning, purpose and death, second-hand information will not do. I cannot survive on second-hand faith in a second-hand God. We have to turn inwards, to look into ourselves, look into this container which is our soul, look and listen to it. Until you have listened to that thing which is dreaming through you, answered the knock on the door in the dark, you will not be able:

> *'To lift this moment in time, in which we*
> *are imprisoned, back again into the level*
> *where the great act of creation is going on.'*
> Sir Laurens van der Post

Our daily lives are our religions. All around us there are opportunities to care, chances to comfort, potential to build, possibilities to love. Everywhere there are doors to open, walls to knock down and bridges to build. The experiences I have drawn on are from the moments in my life that have challenged me but it is in the smallest things that we can find balance. Answering the phone, talking to a stranger, welcoming as a friend, listening to someone when we are in a rush, letting go of a moment of anger, forgiving someone who has let us down or hurt us. It is in the daily steps of the most ordinary things that we find becoming. Spiritual experience is, above all, a practical experience of love. And with love, there are no rules.

THE SEARCH FOR MEANING

*'Every person born into this world represents
something new, something that never existed
before, something original and unique. It is the
duty of every person to know... that there has
never been anyone like him in the world, for if
there had been someone like him there would have
been no need for him to be in the world. Every
single man is a new thing in the world and is
called upon to fulfil his particularity in this world.'*

Martin Buber.

There are many ways to walk through life and many ways to die. I remember once spending the night in the home of an old man. It was in the Turkana Desert on the Sudan border. The old man lived in a tiny round hut the size of a cupboard. All he owned was a ragged blanket and leather sandals. His name was Andat. He was badly emaciated, blind and too weak to eat or drink. He smiled and said that he had had a wonderful life full of good things, a family whom he had loved and enough time to see creation unfold. He told me that he had seen the sunset in a thousand colours

He told me that he had seen the sunset in a thousand colours and the dance of the sky.

and the dance of the sky. Andat had seen his children grow up laughing and now his passing would take his breath unto the wind and he would become part of the great spirit.

'I am not here, I am there.' he whispered...

'I will be the wind, I will be in the rain... I will be with the stars.'

Andat asked only one thing of me; to hold his hand while he changed worlds. That night I sat with him in silence as his last breath fell onto the cold night air and his spirit left him. As I held his hand, I had a profound sense of belonging, of sharing. An awareness of a primal cord that somehow ties us together, in which we are all part of the same energy, the same breath... It has many names.

On another night, many years later, I was called to a slum to visit a mother's child. It was filthy, dark and dangerous. I fell after sliding on open sewage, in waste that children walk in bare feet. It was damp and cold. In a small hovel made from cardboard TV boxes and torn plastic covers, there was a woman squatting in the muck. The smell was suffocating and the child lay on a damp floor with a rancid blanket for a bed. Willis was fifteen and unrecognisable. His skin was grey, his eyes sunken and afraid. I have heard this breathing a thousand times before. I know its rhythm and rattle, the wheezing from the lower lungs and the fragile gasping for air, the open mouth and the whitened tongue. I sat quietly holding Willis' hand which was cold and stiffening.

Willis died that night; the pointless, squalid, shameful death of a child who had no care.

Willis left school about a year ago after getting sick. His mother never had enough money to buy him shoes or medicine, nor to care for his infections or for bus fares to hospital or for food while he got worse. Willis never knew a dignified day in this last year of lying under a putrid cardboard tent. I doubt he ever had a proper meal or a dressed wound or a painless night or an hour free of humiliation. Part of us does not believe it. How can it happen in a world so rich, so full of promise? Willis died that night; the pointless, squalid, shameful death of a child who had no care. A journey that, like so many others, had little to celebrate. His mother stays in her cardboard hut, wondering about tomorrow....

There are many ways to walk through life and many ways to die.

21

Our world does not treat all men as if they were men. We say all men are equal but that depends on where you were born. If you are born black and poor in Africa, you are not equal, you never will be equal. The oppressed do not want the crumbs off our tables when they starve. They do not want CNN cameras in their faces as they weep. They do not ask for white nurses holding up their wasted children for photographers in camps. They want equality, they want respect, they want decency. Over the decades I have seen relief organisations fly in and out of disaster zones and, while the rhetoric and fads change, the fundamental model remains the same. Africa is seen as lesser. It is one example of many. There is something in us that causes us to see others as lesser. She's a woman, he's a Jew, he's a fag, he's black... it is the oldest story in the world.

> *If you are born black and poor in Africa, you are not equal, you never will be equal.*

A friend of mine told me recently a story. Every morning that he went to school he would first throw up in the bathroom. He had knots in his stomach and would frequently cry when he was alone. Jason was a gay teenager in a Dublin school. He was beaten up five times in a single term and would sometimes even hit himself to toughen himself up for the next beating. Finally he was hospitalised after FAG was carved with a knife across his back. He was fifteen.

It is useful to look at a few of the things going on right now on our tiny planet. We don't live in a fair world. We don't even live in a particularly decent world but one that is full of hurt. Our world is in pain. Full of the violence born of emptiness and shame, the madness of broken dreams and lost hope.

Recently there was a 15 year old boy in Western Kenya who had misused his $30 school fees. The boy is tied up with a rope by his father and mother. As the mother hurries out of the family hut in search of a cane, the boy's father douses him with paraffin and sets him on fire. The mother rushes back hearing the screams and finds her son on fire. In another incident, a nursery school

Our world is in pain. Full of the violence born of emptiness and shame, the madness of broken dreams and lost hope.

There are more people alive on planet earth today than all other generations of human beings combined.

The six billion people here are facing the greatest challenges in history.

There are over ten million slaves in the world, more than ever before, and forty million bonded laborers in India.

Over a hundred million people are hungry and there were over a million tons of food thrown away in Europe alone last year.

We spend thirty times more on military expenditure than international development.

In the US, they spend five times more on cosmetics than helping the poor world.

Today across the world ninety million children are labourers, many paid less than 20cts a day.

teacher ties a child to a barbed wire fence and cuts off his finger for stealing a handful of rice. He is starving. She leaves him on the fence.

The first reaction we have to the brutality and scale of suffering in the world is often helplessness. We are overwhelmed by the tidal wave of need and the litany of crises, wars and tragedies. We hear of pointless inanities like this every day and the gradual effect is for us to lose faith in the human spirit, to grow to expect less and less from a species so seemingly devoid of goodness.

Our perception of human problems is often so blinkered that we can only see the anguish and suffering, rarely the simplicity of the solutions. Our very thoughts are weighed down by chains that limit our understanding and vision. Freedom starts with tearing down the walls of the reality we have constructed around us in our heads. When we encounter human pain – a road accident, a depressed friend, a child in tears, a homeless person, we can often feel emotional conflict. It is this tension within us that we need to harmonise into action, turning our angst and worry into positive thought, our sorrow into action and our rage into healing. Yes, we can feel overwhelmed, but it is a lot more useful to feel inspired. Just as our psychological, emotional or physical energies can sometimes become neglected, so too our social and spiritual beings, if left untended, can become underdeveloped and we lose balance in our lives.

Life is full of surprises - some of them fabulous, others hurtful but we are not powerless pawns in a meaningless existence. We are on an epic journey.

When we walk around cities these days, we often go on the streets aware that they are not as safe as they used to be. We are watchful, careful and alert and if we aren't, we probably should be. My own behaviour and attitude when walking around Paris and London led me to challenge some of my assumptions and stereotypes. I had had a growing sense that I was losing touch with some of the realities of my own background. The reality I knew in the West was often confined to giving lectures on ancient tribes, or long evenings by the fire sipping red wine listening to music. Restaurants, art exhibitions, the gym, bookshops. I would try to get a feel for different currents by reading magazines from every age group; from comics and teen magazines to heavy metal and computer weekly's. I joined both the Labour party and the Conservative party, then other groups. I became proactive in web sites and advice lines providing support to kids who were depressed. It was important for me to be in touch with what was happening in my own country.

Opening our minds can be painful as we start to recognise the limitations in the way we think.

Once though, instead of a ten-day retreat in an enclosed monastery, I decided to spend the time living rough on the streets of London without any money. It was strange becoming completely invisible to passers by. Not only were we ignored, we were unseen. It was odd how people's faces would change into a sort of underground rush hour expression as they walked by.

The first few days were just freezing, I never quite got used to the cold but as I began to find places to stay under bridges, in Selfridges doorway, around the back of Victoria station, I met more and more people who were sleeping rough. I had held the notion that I would be meeting tramps and beggars, rejects and mental patients – the unwanted and the dysfunctional but the thing one discovers about being on the street is that there is a totally separate subculture alive and thriving. There is a hierarchy, there are places that are safe and those that are not. The array of people you meet ranges from those who had run away from middle class homes to the safety of the street, wives that had been beaten, young kids who had often been hurt or simply just screamed at and never listened to, to the many who had just had a series of bad breaks. There are the short termers who will live a few weeks rough until they can find something else, the medium termers who have been around a year or so and people like Jed, who once bought me a Big Mac and gave me a piece of plastic to sleep on. He had been around for eleven years and looked it. Sleeping rough in London is very different to sleeping rough in Paris. In Paris don't even try it, it's dangerous.

It's hard to know where to start looking for sense.

When you change the script of your days, step out of your context and away from the familiar, it can be very scary. There are many of life's surprises that can put us on the 'streets', outside the routine comfort zones that provide us with the securities we need. Whether you sleep out on the streets, get very sick or come out of a wounding relationship, you are left disorientated, without reference points, sometimes without anchors. If you lose your job, scar your face, fall outside the norm in any of a thousand ways, people look at you differently, treat you in a new way. Life is full of surprises – some of them fabulous, others hurtful but we are not powerless pawns in a meaningless existence. We are on an epic journey.

Sometimes the bloodiness of humanity can even leave us bored, indifferent, untouched.

This journey is deeply influenced by the people we listen to, the things we are swayed by and the choices we make. We are innately tribal – we like the familiar, we like to belong. This in itself can blind us. Who is this guy? He's black, he's gay, he's a drunk... Our expectations can distort how we see and talk to people. Our pre-judgements and pre-conceived ideas can also limit our ability to be ourselves. Opening our minds can be painful as we start to recognise the limitations in the way we think. So too, our emotional history brings to each experience the biases, prejudices and residue of everything we have tasted before. If I haul my broken heart into my next relationship or wait for the failures of the past to emerge in my future, I will make very narrow choices in my tomorrows.

Learning involves listening and risking, discovering new paths, being creative and unlearning assumptions. There is a Maasai saying:

> *'May you see what you see through*
> *different eyes, may you hear with different*
> *ears, may you taste what you have never*
> *tasted and go further than yourself.'*

I was talking to a child in Bombay who was sold to a man by her parents because their crop had failed and they could not find food. Most of the year they worked as their parents did, on the fields of their landlord without pay, just to be allowed to live in the village. The parents of Nedha had to sell her to pay off the family debt to the landlord for the year. Nedha works near the railway lines and has been used by four or five men a day for the last two years. As she walked into the hot sticky night past the rickshaws towards the side streets, she turned and waved and I wondered what the hell are we all doing. I doubted if the money I gave her would be used to return to Northern India. Twelve-year-old girls should have a better childhood.

One of the things we pick up fast as we grow up is that everything is not OK. Then we often realise that we ourselves

29

are not OK, and that our circumstances or family life is not what we might want or need. Sometimes life is not all it promised to be and yet I believe that when love pervades the way in which we see ourselves there is a profound, inexplicable change in the way we engage life. It is as though the world around us transforms and while everything might still not be perfect, life changes so dynamically that it alters the very process of experience, creating a chain reaction in our lives. As we mature, we try and sort out what's good for us, what's bad, and more or less make sense of the ordinariness of our daily lives. We need to have a purpose in our lives, no matter how unprocessed or unspoken this feeling is. We need to belong, to be fulfilled.

To die of AIDS in Africa is, for many thousands of people, an intensely humiliating ordeal, slow... obscene.

There is something in all of us that desires contentment and an inclination to believe in something, someone. We want to feel the true meaning of love. For many, these impulses lie unspoken at the pit of our guts. A questioning that may remain unresolved throughout our lives. It is man's search for purpose – our search for meaning.

It's hard to know where to start looking for sense. The bloodiness of humanity can fill us with tears, the map of our experience can teach us to be careful and we are becoming increasingly conditioned to be afraid. It's easy to be doubtful and sceptical as we look around us. It's a big world out there – all the pain in it is not my fault, and I can't absorb all the crazy things that happen. Sometimes the bloodiness of humanity can even leave us bored, indifferent, untouched.

Is there a way in which they can inspire us to change the way we see the world – to engage it, challenge it. To become part of the solution rather than an observer who feels sorrow.

It is only when someone we love is in pain or afraid that we wake from our complacency. Only when the number becomes a person does the newspaper article becomes a tragedy, a tragedy like Atria...

Atria is a 17 year old boy who, a year before his death, weighs 7 stone. He is afraid and has left his village. His pulse is rapid and he is nervous, he is ashamed, he is sweating, he is embarrassed to be here.

He has bad headaches and can't sleep well. He tries to smile but his hands are trembling. The problem isn't the rashes or the intestinal worms. They are easily cleared up but it's not as simple to clear up the anger and the fear or the sleepless nights or the panic attacks. How long a few minutes can be... the sense of powerlessness seeing your body fall away from you, the humiliation of disintegrating. Some infections are harder to deal with – a mouth filled with ulcers, an inflamed penis, the difficulty shitting and urinating.

As the disease progresses so too does the nausea, the back pain and the aching. The muscle cramps always hurt, especially when there's very little muscle. Atria is a beautiful man with stunning eyes, fading slowly, thinness becoming a skeletal grey haunting waste... he has severe diarrhoea and the dull aches in his stomach become sharp pains. Despite the best of efforts, he becomes anaemic and sight fades, so too does concentration. Atria has stinging burning pain from urinary tract infections which hurt as his urinary tract becomes blood red and raw. Excreting has become a feared ordeal as his anus has lost its muscular contraction and often gets infected. He has no buttocks, just stretched skin over a pelvic bone that is sore to lie on. His joints are hypersensitive. Above all Atria has difficulty breathing. It's a horrible wheezing gurgling that stops him sleeping and he moans a lot because the painkillers are useless.

He was a proud energetic guy, very popular and ambitious, with a deadly sense of fun. Most of all he hates the fact that he leaks and drips, smells badly and often cannot control his bowel movements or urination. He gets really angry at himself. Headaches are constant and he is weak and gets very dizzy. He cannot eat easily as his enzymes are breaking down and his ability to digest is deteriorating. Atria bruises easily and the slightest knock is very sore and painful.

We might not be able to feed the starving, but we might be able to feed one person.

He is now 6 stone. After another few weeks the boy is very drained. His mouth is full of oral thrush, a white fungus over his tongue and gums. His mouth has a lot of ulcers and he has difficulty swallowing. Breathing is increasingly difficult and laboured. By now, pneumonia is ravaging his ruined body. All movement is acutely painful and distressing. The intestinal worms are back again... Atria's limbs are stiffening and his back is covered in large sores. These are ulcers that leak and bleed but do not heal; they are very distressing and impossible to manage in a small hut. His buttocks have gone. There is only flaccid skin drawn over a gaping hole. The hole is raw and inflamed like a small doughnut. Excreting is now no longer painful as sensations are dying. It is a long and slow experience. Sometimes his colon sticks out of his anus as there is no muscle or sphincter to protect his bowels. To die of AIDS in Africa is, for many thousands of people, an intensely humiliating ordeal, slow... obscene.

There is a profound insecurity at the heart of any consumer society because it creates needs and expectations where there aren't any

The issues that need to be addressed are those of controlling the pain, managing the distress, reducing the humiliation, the creation of dignity in extreme situations as well as reducing the multiple infections and risk of cross infection to children... But the biggest issue of all is loneliness.

Atria is now in his last days of life. His tear ducts have dried up, his hair has fallen out, his bones are brittle. He has no muscle or fat and his heart is 70% weaker than pre HIV. He has been eaten alive by repeated assaults on his body and has no resistance. All Atria's senses are shutting down. His skin is blistered and scaly as scabs cannot form .His finger and toenails have fallen out. The bedsores and ulcers have spread, becoming sources of multiple deep infection. Breathing is almost impossible and the slightest movement is slow and full of dreadful anxiety. I give him water drop by drop through a straw. I hold his frail stiffened hand, he is cold, he has no tears. I look into his eyes... I whisper to him and kiss him... He slowly inhales, half closes his eyes... he breathes out, very slowly...

The flow of energy is about how we live.

Atria's face relaxes, the tormented body loosens......... he has gone.

I held him in my arms and wept.

I do not think there is any meaning in cruelty or the pain of the innocent. So should this boy's story and the other stories shared here create in us feelings of futility, despair and frustration? Or is there another reality? Is there a way in which they can inspire us to change the way we see the world – to engage it, challenge it. To become part of the solution rather than an observer who feels sorrow.

I have never particularly felt the need to explain things. I have always thought that the Western preoccupation with needing to have explanations was very limiting.

Human experiences rarely make sense, are often random and we waste a lot of energy trying to rationalise things that exist outside reason. We can react to human anguish either by externalising it, or by reaching out. We can each choose what to do and that is

Whether we live among the old tribes of the Northern deserts or we live in London and have just fallen in love, the new things happening around us can be disturbing and provoking.

the point. We can make a difference. Each of us really can change the world. We might not be able to feed the starving, but we might be able to feed one person.

When I was growing up, I couldn't really care about being part of a solution as I just did not see the problem related to me. My own view of the world did not cry at the suffering on the planet. The violence on the news, which I never watched anyway, was always somewhere else. I was a happy positive guy surrounded by caring friends and we were all really optimistic, good hearted and upbeat. But was that the full story? Was my world really that together and sorted?

We are all in some way afraid of the future – we do not know what tomorrow will bring. We are afraid of risk, of pain, of failure. Sometimes reality pours in the floodgates of our own horizons. Those things that always happen to someone else one day happen in our lives, bringing tomorrow crashing in on us in an earthquake of shattered dreams. The love we have received in our lives helps to encounter the surprises of life. If we had been deeply damaged, we would be too afraid to take any risks. It would be easier to withdraw into ourselves for everything in life that has meaning involves risk and the potential for pain. We fall in love, we have children, we strive to do our best, we make choices. In everything we risk failure, and yet without making friends, exploring, being in love, life can be very solitary.

We can only be our true selves when we accept ourselves, and are accepted, completely just as we are.

The essence of life is change. This might be gradual deterioration or decay, or it might be dynamic creativity, but nevertheless it is change. Some people age and become bitter and sour, others become so infused with energy and life that they fill everyone around them with goodness. When we try to protect ourselves by avoiding life, by not encountering growth, we become ill. It is this attempt to avoid legitimate suffering that lies at the root of all emotional illness. It is healthy to embrace the new, the different, the alien, the strange. We must continually revise our maps

Real love enlarges rather than diminishes the self; it fills the self rather than depleting it.

and sometimes, when enough new information has been gathered, we must make major revisions. If we do not, our search for meaning becomes a retreat from the risk of being alive.

When I was growing up we played and roamed in a way that children don't today. We have become uneasy in ourselves, anxious about the future and in that angst dwells the ghosts of dread and the whispers of failure.

There is a profound insecurity at the heart of any consumer society because it creates needs and expectations where there aren't any and, at the same time, dissatisfaction with what we do have. Within a value system that measures us by what we own and what we earn, the seeds of emptiness are sown. Our world, so driven by buying, having, getting, undermines our sense of self worth and our ability to become and be whole. What is sold to us as happiness is often part of a cycle of insatiable consumerism that drives an economy dependent on creating a constant need for more. These things are often the paths to deep anxiety and stress, not happiness. And we pass it on. We are conditioning our children to swim in a culture of 'having' and 'possessing' and it is not bringing them joy. It is pointing them in the wrong direction. True happiness has its origins somewhere else.

He was the future of what Africa should be; dynamic, intelligent, exciting, stunning, gifted, creative.

Few people, rich or poor, make the most of what they possess. In their anxiety to increase the amount of means for future enjoyment, they are apt to lose sight of the capability of them for the present. Above all, they overlook the thousand things to enjoy which lie round about them, free to everybody, and obtainable by the very willingness to be pleased. I think that this is what Eastern thought sees as lifestyle blocking energy. The flow of energy is about how we live. Whether we use a Western scientific model or a Buddhist perception, it is about the energy within us.

The places I eat, the company I keep, the web sites I access, the people I relax with, those I live with, the work I do, the things I read – these, and countless other things, effect my 'me' and my understanding of my world. We create a world born from our experiences and construct a reality in which meaning is defined by familiar reference points. This is how we deal with the world – by making choices, setting the horizons and boundaries, defining goals, selecting within our means from endless possibilities.

In order to preserve our view of the world around us, we need to filter out those things that do not fit into our reality. We cannot absorb everything so we make choices. We sometimes shut out noisy neighbours or ideas that disturb us, we instinctively select the things that we are most comfortable and familiar with. In time, we develop opinions, ideas and beliefs, often conditioned by our immediate family and peer group. Most people, most of the time, tend to construct their view of things this way and, to a large extent, how we deal with everything is closely linked to this thought process. Our senses feed into

His efforts to maintain a normal existence met with a thousand falls on the road to his calvary.

this reality and we interpret meaning and truth through the parameters we have been encultured in and conditioned to. But our world is often shattered by a whole range of experiences that don't suit the script or the software we think in. Whatever our thought process, we can struggle to deal with intrusions that don't fit our perception of the world.

Whether we live among the old tribes of the Northern

deserts or we live in London and have just fallen in love, the new things happening around us can be disturbing and provoking. Old reference points and standards of behaviour no longer apply so we often look outside our immediate experience for role models or inspiration but we have no heroes any more, only celebrities. Entertainers and footballers have replaced greatness. Our appetite for celebrity and peoples' private lives reflect the emptiness in our society. It is in private life that we can now find the great characters for they are too great to get into the public world.

If we are not in touch with the light, we become lost and afraid. We can look for things to fill us, but only the light can complete us.

What do we seek? I believe that we are all looking for the same thing. Whether we be students or businessmen, prostitutes or priests – we are looking as best as we can for this same thing. I think we are in search of being our deeper selves. We can only be our true selves when we accept ourselves, and are accepted, completely just as we are. It is in the healing power of that acceptance that we are made whole, complete. The things we do in life are frequently our own efforts to disown this wholeness for we have rarely been taught the truth, the extraordinary truth about ourselves. We have been taught to conform, taught to think in straight lines, to see only the visible, to imagine only little things. We have learnt to diminish others and be persuaded of our own lack of worth.

In the illusion of the modern world, people are measured by passing things; what they wear, how they appear, what structure they live in, how many things they have collected, where they live, what colour they are. These are so irrelevant but they can distract people their whole lifetimes.

Know that the things we call joy, happiness and meaning are our often-frustrated search for love. By love I mean the willingness to extend one's self for the purpose of nurturing one's own or another's self. This is a self-replenishing act because it has no strings. It is without condition. Real love enlarges rather than diminishes the self; it fills the self rather than depleting it. The moment we attach conditions to this love, it becomes something else and we start to invest our energies into the manipulation of ourselves or the other person into roles in our movie, in our perception of how things should be. When we do this we cannot find happiness because happiness is generated by emptying ourselves, not by trying to satisfy our perceived needs. It is in such a love that we find belonging.

For many years I have worked with the dying. Many of us have helped set up training workshops for communities now facing the pandemic of AIDS across parts of East Africa. It meant preparing often illiterate, overworked mothers for the kind of tasks an intensive care unit would do in Europe... the management and care of the severely sick and terminally ill, like Sammy.

He lies in a pool of his own fluid, he struggles for breath and is unable to speak. His wasted limbs are taut and cold, his hands and feet contracted. His beautiful face has become a macabre mask. He is withered, afraid, alone, ridden with disease, his tongue layered in thick green scum. Sammy tried to turn towards me, he could only manage to move his eyes slightly, he could not see me. But he managed to reach his arms towards me... He could no longer cry for his tear ducts has dried and he whispered 'take me home'. He would tell me later how he felt he was not worth loving, not worth anything. Once he looked into a mirror and had nightmares. His hospital bed was filthy, he was grey, afraid, unable to eat. He knew he was dying but did not want to die here, now, this way. I covered his nakedness

I remember feeling two things. A very deep sense of gratitude for my life and an excitement that I might be changing worlds.

with my coat and lifted him in my arms... The last time I had done so was seventeen years before when he was six years old and he wanted to climb a tree to pick mangoes. I carried Sammy to the car and held him on the back seat in my arms.

Once there was so much life in him. He was the future of what Africa should be; dynamic, intelligent, exciting, stunning, gifted, creative. Now a few months later, in the final hours of his life as it was mercilessly stripped from him, Sammy was not a brave man. He hated hospitals, fainted at the sight of blood, and was very sensitive. The months he spent reaching this point were horrific with many sleepless nights, ghosts, nightmares. His efforts to maintain a normal existence met with a thousand falls on the road to his calvary.

The days I lay in that hut in the remote Savannah were a wonderful journey into trust.

I remember the first time his hair started to fall out, the first time he had difficulty walking and the times he would fall and the wounds would not heal. He would hide his foul breath from his daughter and when she would leap into his embrace, he would not show the physical pain it gave him to hold her. One afternoon I was feeding him water through a straw and he looked up at me.

'Its enough... I'm ready now.'

'Yes Sammy, it's time isn't it'. I kissed his cold grey scalp for there were no lips left, just wounds and an hour later he left the ruins of his tortured body and became light.

We search for meaning, for a reason to live and a reason to die. We question, we explore. There are some, however, who believe there are no issues to explore and a great many who hold the view that it is unnecessary to question many of the dynamics and social realities around us. I have friends who are atheists, others who are agnostics. I know people who have real problems with the idea of introducing the mystical or the spiritual into the inquiry but if we are not in touch with the light, we become lost and afraid. We can look for things to fill us, but only the light can complete us.

Sometimes we get so caught up in our own edition of reality that we lose contact with what is actually happening.

I have been close to death five times. On three of those occasions I had the last rites which, in the Catholic tradition, are the preparation for death, a saying farewell to the visible and a welcoming of the invisible. Once during a cholera epidemic, I was living on the plains among the Maasai nomads of Northern Tanzania. We had been in the midst of meetings and clinics, on long walks through the bush and had had long nights travelling from homestead to homestead. The nights were awe inspiring as the heavens were brightly lit with a billion stars and the sound of Africa filled us with majesty and delight.

One afternoon, I felt very tired and went to lie down in our cow dung hut. As I lay there, I began feeling a coldness come across my body and a cloud over my vision. I was conscious of losing control of my legs and arms and as I lay there my eyes dimmed and finally all light passed into nothingness. I had gone blind. I was now very cold, but not feverish and my breathing was even. My Maasai friends arrived and we decided, as I was the only one able to drive, to stay where we were. During the hours that followed I became worse, my breathing became erratic and other symptoms appeared, not least a fever, a swelling of the limbs and crescent rashes over my body. It was only the following morning when I awoke still completely blind and breathing with great difficulty that I realised that I might be dying. I was getting rapidly worse with swollen glands, muscular contractions and fever.

The days I lay in that hut in the remote Savannah were a wonderful journey into trust.

As I lay in the hut, I remember feeling two things. A very deep sense of gratitude for my life and an excitement that I might be changing worlds. This excitement was full of a curiosity as to what it would be like being present to the unseen. There was no flashing of my life before my eyes, no anxiety, just a quiet pleasure. This enthralment eclipsed the physical state I was in and I was preoccupied with the sense of a presence and a readiness to let go of the gift of Life. It had been a beautiful journey.

In death, the only person leaving your body is you. It is something no one can do for you, no matter how much tenderness and love they have for you. We have to leave alone... at least so I thought. But no person dies alone. There was a calmness in me, a trust. It was not just faith. It was more a complete and utter pleasure in knowing, from some deep part of the light within, that the presence and love and energy and calm of the Sacred was there. Some things are incommunicable, ineffable, totally beyond words. The power of love, the tenderness a mother has for her baby, the emotions one has for the beloved, the extent you would go to for your child.

It was like being struck between the eyes only slowly, penetrating sound, just noise and a blurred black everywhere shaking and moving violently.

In the same way the depth and wave of grace that poured within me as I lay in a terrible mess on the ground had no words. The days I lay in that hut in the remote Savannah were a wonderful journey into trust. I had no medication and was lucid the entire time, surrounded by friends, not least a Maasai grandmother who put water on my swollen lips drop by drop, for hours at a time and kept the flies away. I have had some sense of what it is to let go of life this side of existence and I know that how people are cared for and valued during their last months and moments is of real importance.

The strange thing about us is that we so often forget to enjoy ourselves. We get so caught up in worrying when worry will not change anything. We become so anxious about outcomes and results, deadlines and certitudes that we cannot live without them.

I sat under a tree one-day with an old man in the Sudan. He sat for a long time and then said, 'You know the problem with people who run around is they can't wait for things to sort themselves out. They look at the earth and say, do this. They look at a problem and run around it but the universe will handle the details because nature unfolds perfectly without us. If we trust and let go, the magic of what is inside will work.' I think the old man was right. Sometimes we get so caught up in our own edition of reality that we lose contact with what is actually happening. We need to be constantly awoken into mystery, surprised by joy.

I remember once being camped on the Savannah plains north of Kilimanjaro. We were on foot and had vaccinated over a thousand children in a single week. We were on a roll. It was about three in the morning and the night was pitch black apart from the countless stars that one can see from these plains that stretch a thousand miles. I was lying on my back looking up at the hypnotic symphony of space reflecting

If we are ready to tear down the walls that confine us, break the cage that imprisons us, we will discover what our wings are for.

countless silent ions of light and sound and galaxies. I was mesmerised by the vastness, lost for words to embrace the scale of awe-inspiring breadth and majesty of the sky.

There is nowhere quite as silent as the equatorial sub Sahara on the great plains; nowhere quite as untouched. I was drifting into the unspeakable beauty when thunder, lightening, earthquake… the ground trembled under my body and I was shaken. The warriors with me jumped up and dragged me to my feet, 'iltomea, iltomea'.

I was gathering my senses like you see people do in freeze-frame films, it was slow motion, then suddenly all around us was black motion. There was crashing and breaking, and trees being ripped asunder. It was like being struck between the eyes only slowly, penetrating sound, just noise and a blurred black everywhere shaking and moving violently. The baleful sounds began to define themselves into howls, no, not howls more wailing, a deep, heavy baying. The blackness that was making me choke became dark deep red suffocation, clouds of dust, panic, confusion, 'iltomea'.

The core of who we are is born in the daily moments of ordinary living.

What? What word is that? My mind was distracted by fear, dazed by the stars. I was choking, coughing, spluttering, deafened. The red dust filled my nostrils, I could barely breath as if caught in some paralysing asthmatic attack,

I was remembering, remembering what language,? What word? Iltomea,... ahh, shit, yes... elephants... It was like being inside a film that you could see on the big screen. This just was not happening, could not be happening, just how did I get here? What the hell am I doing? I want to go home... get me out of here... then at the height of the earthquake as I was thinking we would all be pounded into ant fodder, the sky lost under a thick cloud of alluvial red dust, there was a breath, the pounding of hearts, the very loud pounding of hearts, and then the distant trumpeting of the herd as it tore away from us and through the undergrowth obliterating everything in it's wake.

We stood numb for maybe five minutes. I didn't notice the blood on my hand or the smashed camp. I was only conscious of the amazing sound of breath in my body and the thumping of my heart. We were alive. Our camp was no longer detectable, the glade levelled but the five of us were miraculously unscathed. It was fully an hour before we looked up again from the havoc that lay about us and there, even more breathtaking than ever, was the same infinity, the same boundless vistas of the universe, still, untroubled, unfolding.

There are a few things as awe inspiring as lying out in the African Bush. I often stare at the stars – on the great plains the ferment is a linking mass of activity. Everything is visible – billions of stars light up the sky and the bright darkness pulsates with wonder. As you lie gazing upwards you sense two things – firstly how tiny and minuscule we are in the vastness of the cosmos. Secondly – how much a part of the fabric of creation we are as we draw breath. This sense of cosmic scale and oneness can be seen in the tapestry of our daily lives. The invincible power of nature and the unfolding of the universe dances all around us.

The six billion people here are facing the greatest challenges in history.

Our moment on an elephant trail in a tiny part of a speck on the African plains had not disturbed what ought to be. And I realised in that moment that, because of the dread and absorption we have in the little dramas of each day, it is easy for us to lose sight of the big picture. Easy to lose ourselves in the small print, and forget that there is a greater truth, a larger symmetry which is already in harmony. Sometimes we get distracted by the dust, the noise, the clouds, the movement and, for the best reasons in the world, we lose sight of reality.

How we get up each morning depends a lot on our attitude. How we search for meaning also depends on the way we see ourselves and the world around us. If we are looking for the kind of inspiration that won't change the way we live, we will get just that. But if we are ready to tear down the walls that confine us, break the cage that imprisons us, we will discover what our wings are for.

We have to begin by completely letting go of the past, having no fear of the future and filling today with the whole of ourselves with abandon and innocence. Walt Disney often spoke of leaps in your imagination, creating your fantasies, becoming your dreams and then some. In an interview shortly before his death, he laughed and commented 'it's kind of fun doing the impossible'. The core of who we are is born in the daily moments of ordinary living. It is here we must always renew our vision, our passion, our state of becoming. The magic of discovering, growing, evolving, is all about risking. If we are always in the same place with the same people and doing the same things we limit ourselves to the familiar. So too if we limit the way we think, the horizons of our dreams and the possibilities of our actions, we can become human bonsais. So ask:

What is within my heart?
What is worth living for?
What is more precious than life?
What is worth dying for?
What is sacred?
What is the spirit made of?

If you think of everything that is utterly precious to you, absolutely essential to you – you will find that it is all invisible. Tenderness, breath, belonging, trust, love. It is with this discovery that the journey changes into something else, that we are no longer alone, that we are part of something else, something bigger. If we align our thoughts, emotions, and actions with the highest part of ourselves, we will become filled with enthusiasm, purpose, and meaning. It is this passion and drive that engages us in the full chaos, delight and drama of living.

Somewhere in that space is the time
we taste what we truly live, believe, are.
There lies our living creed,
the things we live our lives by.
You will never be happy if you continue
to search for what happiness consists of.
You will never live if you are looking for
the meaning of life.
Camus

The Dance

*'If you wish to glimpse inside a human soul and
get to know a man, don't bother analysing his
ways of being silent, of talking, of weeping, or
seeing how much he is moved by noble ideas;
you'll get better results if you just watch him
laugh. If he laughs well, he's a good man.'*

The Adolescent, Dostoevsky

I used to like my world, the familiar, the safe. When it was
possible to imagine a life with no fear, no pain, no anguish.
Like many people I had no idea of how utterly unimaginable
human poverty can get. I had heard the words, but they did
not prepare me for the reality. Poverty revolts me, so does
suffering.

I run a series of medical programmes in Africa, the charity I founded originally started as a response to the hunger and suffering in desert areas of the sub Sahara. The friends who help in this work are scattered across many countries so we called our charity the International community for relief of starvation and suffering, ICROSS for short. As part of our efforts to reach neglected and vulnerable children, I had been spending a growing amount of time with children who have fallen off the scale of extreme poverty and are now somewhere outside of our imagination. I visited a child who lives in an unused drain with her brother behind a railway track. Saine is ten, Dan is six. She is one of the growing number of children orphaned by AIDS – her mother died a few months ago. Saine has never had a home, never slept in a bed. She has never had a hot bath, never been to school or played with a toy or known the most basic things we assume are part of existence.

I imagined myself at ten years old – my toys, my friends, my favourite TV programmes – above all, the safety and security of a world full of affection and delight.

Saine sleeps on old plastic sheeting, does not own a pair of shoes and begs for food every day. Dan is very underweight, stunted and afraid of the dark. They wash in a polluted river full of rubbish. Both these children have scabies, intestinal worms and lice. Saine and Dan were with their mother when she died and had looked after her in the last weeks of her illness. At six and ten, they have had to endure more anguish than most of us see in our lifetimes. As I walked away, waving to the two grins shining behind me, I realised the scale of the divide between us. All children are equal but some truly are more equal than others.

There are perhaps many paths to truth, to happiness, many ways to find our way home, but in my deeper self I doubt if any of them can exist without Saine and Dan. Unless there is room in our reality to embrace and touch the lives of those who have no chance without us, unless we reach out our hands from our world and touch the lives of those whose worlds we cannot begin to comprehend, we deny something essential in ourselves. As I think of my own life and the lives of those I love and care about, I am silenced and drawn to wonder about our own reality, a reality not shared by all.

We have recently been able to help Saine and Dan, who are now at school, cared for, loved and have hope.

We make ourselves real by knowing the truth and telling the truth.

In many parts of Africa, traditional realities have imploded hastened by extremes of poverty – whole social networks have collapsed. Many countries are in the throes of their own self annihilation and the ruins of classrooms still have children's remains lying unburied on the floors. Even within tribes there is rarely harmony, and the myth of the extended family has long been shattered as entire nations struggle to deal with the forty million children orphaned.

Saine sleeps on old plastic sheeting, does not own a pair of shoes and begs for food every day.

In the Western world, there is a strong vein of negativity that pervades thought like a grey cloud blocking the sun. It is an attitude that permeates everything. I have never seen this energy in Africa, except in the corridors of power. It seems to like cold places. It can be seen in the media and in advertising, in shop windows and etched on faces in the high street. It helps to shatter and ultimately destroy our most precious non-material possessions: confidence in the existence of meaningful purposes of human activity and respect for the integrity of man.

This set of perceptions embraces a thought process that depreciates emotion, drags them down and diminishes beauty. It is an impatient way of life, pressured and worried – it characterises the desert of the modern city. Here, materialism is one of life's surrogates. We collect things, buy things, possess things. We usually have much more than we really need but our culture and conditioning programme us to think about buying all the time. Marketing and advertising are inherently dishonest because they feed the vulnerability and inadequacies of targeted groups to buy things that are rarely needed.

Success, progress and achievement are closely linked to ownership of certain types of things. Kids need the latest designer trainers, the latest CD. The fever of advertising depends on conditioning people to want – and finally believe that they need. Football teams and boy bands generate half their profits from merchandise. Peer pressure and well-managed advertising creates needs and fuels market demand. All the reasoning in the world won't dissuade a kid from not wanting to be the only one in her class without the latest CD player.

> *Marketing and advertising are inherently dishonest because they feed the vulnerability and inadequacies of targeted groups to buy things that are rarely needed.*

Socrates never tried to persuade his followers to live simply but for himself, he owned nothing and had only the clothes he stood up in. He would sometimes go to the market and see what the merchants were selling. When asked why he would reply 'I enjoy seeing all the things I am happy without'. Perhaps we need to think more about what we do not need or, as Mother Teresa said, learn the meaning of 'enough'.

It is here too that much anxiety comes from the culture of worshipping the future – you will become thin eventually, desired after you possess the latest fashion, sexy after you buy the latest jeans. You will be successful when you qualify, you can live your life after you graduate. Millions of people are deceived by the lies of a world that does not value its children as it should.

We should be telling our children to live now, to celebrate the wonder of life here at this moment. It is destructive to imagine happiness exists somewhere in the future. Happiness is born here, this instant, we do not need to wait. The poverty of our world is not that we don't have money but that we don't have dreams. Time, it is so precious. The smallest moments are irreplaceable. When St Francis Xavier said 'be great in little things', I think he echoed Buddha in his call to celebrate the 'now' with the whole of your 'YES' otherwise we live in a state without joy with a world view without the promise of life, without the human spirit. One which sees stress and fear in everything through a narrow archway where the individual dwells alone, solitary, suspicious, defensive.

Millions of people are deceived by the lies of a world that does not value its children as it should.

Our cities can be lonely, often isolating, places. So too can our places of learning and work be. Hell was described by the poet, mystic and monk Thomas Merton as a place where no one has anything in common with anybody else except the fact that they all hate one another and cannot get away from one another and from themselves. A place where they are all thrown together in the fire and each one tries to thrust the other away from him with

So much of how we behave is based on fear, fear of rejection.

a huge, impotent hatred. And the reason why they want to be free of one another is not so much that they hate what they see in others as that they think others hate what they see in them: and all recognise in one another what they detest in themselves – selfishness and impotence, agony, terror and despair. This is a great description of social failure and of conflict. So much of what we say and do is in anticipation of how others will judge us, what they will say. So much of how we behave is based on fear, fear of rejection. The despair in our world springs from inner pain, whether solitary or collective.

My own experience of brutality and cruelty has taught me that the people who are violent and angry are like Merton's people in the fire – full of self destruction. I remember seeing the half-living bodies of children tied to wooden floats coming ashore on Lake Victoria – horribly mutilated and dismembered, veins tied to prolong their agony. In Rwanda, over a million human beings were murdered in that orgy of violence, the truth of which cannot be put into words.

For over a year, we counselled a young UN peacekeeper who had served in Bosnia. The raw evil he saw broke his heart. Soldiers had gone into schools and raped girls, shot teachers, made boys castrate each other with their teeth, nailed students to the blackboards and then left. The young soldier had seen mass graves and the bodies of mothers still enfolded around their children as they tried to comfort and protect them. The prosecutor in one of the war crimes tribunals broke down in tears reading the litany of charges, each worse than the rest. As with so many things, the scale of the atrocities remains inconceivable, as unbelievable as the factories built to liquidate the Jews in Nazi Germany. What is very difficult to imagine, doesn't exist.

There are many versions of the story of a young woman in a concentration camp. Which camp is unimportant for I am sure there are such prisoners in most camps and prisons and Gulags. In this concentration camp, the prisoners had been tortured and broken, abused and starved. Guards would amuse themselves seeing how long children would take to suffocate and watch while they drowned prisoners in freezing water.

When Maria arrived in the camp, she saw the horror and the clouds of hell about her. Her clothes had been removed and she had been given dark grey prison rags that reeked of the sweat and fear of the prisoner who had worn them before her. Her beautiful cascading hair was sheared off and her scalp scratched and scraped from the brutal humiliation

A thousand faces lifted from the damp boards as they heard the sound rising above the darkness to the stars.

of being shaved. She was given a number and was a person no longer. Just a thing, less than a thing, an inconvenience taking up space in a world better off without her.

One evening Maria stood in the middle of the camp and, trembling slightly, lifted her violin and began playing the most wonderful concerto. For a moment the camp stopped, wondering where the heavenly music came from then two guards came and kicked her, slapped her on the face and dragged her off warning her not to play again. The next evening she was there. Maria stood defiantly in the middle of the camp and played for what she thought was the last time. She put all her heart in those few moments before the guards came and, for a time, Mozart's magic filled the darkness and sang the most glorious harmony of the angels, reminding those cowering in fear, of a greatness and a beauty.

The guards dragged Maria away and her screams could be heard long into the night. For weeks she was not seen and life in the camp returned to the sounds of labour, whips, cries and the harsh orders barked at lines of numbered prisoners.

One night all that could be heard was the rain pelting on the iron roofs and the sentries with their dogs behind the stone walls. But then through the wind and the coughing of broken men could be heard a single note, a strange note, but a note that took shape in the darkness nevertheless. A thousand faces lifted from the damp boards as they heard the sound rising above the darkness to the stars. Maria was playing. She had a single string. That afternoon she had been released from the filthy cell where she had been raped and her fingers cut off. The bleeding broken young woman poured out her whole self in that single sweet note and even as the dogs closed in about her she smiled and every heart in the camp was awake, every guard raged and every star danced in the heavens.

In everything we are, there is the potential to bring joy or sadness – each drawn from the well that is our heart.

I think it was Booker Washington who said 'I will not permit any man to narrow and degrade my soul by making me hate him.'

In Kenya there is practice of beating to death or torching thieves who are all too often merely innocent bystanders. On one occasion I came across a boy being beaten by a crowd. He was accused of stealing bananas. Nine bananas to be precise. The boy had already been tied, beaten with sticks and an old car tire had been put around his neck. The mob were now kicking the struggling boy who was screaming for mercy. He could no longer pronounce any words as his mouth was full of blood and his screaming was stifled by the kicks.

As luck would have it, I was in a Land Rover visiting a group of women who care for abandoned children. I drove up as close as possible and slowly got out of the car. The crowd were fuelling each other's hysteria. I eased my *Saying hello to the Maasai is a finely nuanced activity.* way through them and eventually placed myself beside the boy who was then pulled away from me by his head. I had a small fire extinguisher in my hand that I hung onto. The two Maasai grandmothers I was with also pushed through the crowd and pulled the boy back towards me by his bloodied legs. A man, who was almost catatonic with rage, began splashing the boy with petrol and shouting so wildly that no one knew what he was saying. They weren't even his bananas.

I kept talking calmly - asking the group to calm down. The old Maasai who were with me were composed too which helped greatly. I stood completely over the boy as the crowd became less frenzied. Then the hysterical man lit a match and told me to get away. As he threw the match I saw the line of flames out the corner of my eyes. Adrenaline and a primal urge for self preservation hurled me to one side in what skiers call a flying side leap. The Maasai did not move but simply stood by the boy. It was really their quiet courage and dignity that saved him. I aimed the foam jet at the base of the flames turning him into a snowman and did not stop until the can was empty. It was then the women in the crowd began berating the man who nearly set the old women on fire. As it turned out, the man who wanted to set the boy on fire was the one who did take the bananas.

If you came across a child with severe malnutrition, you gave the child's mother a goat.

As we drove the boy to hospital, I observed the two Maasai grandmothers. Their voices were even, completely calm, as if nothing had happened. I was drenched in sweat. They didn't even miss a heart beat. It was only on our way back to Maasailand that I noticed that the foot of one of the women was blistered badly from being caught in the fire. I expressed concern at the angry wound but she laughed and said:

> *'It's only there if you feel it. If you don't put it in your mind, it doesn't exist'.*

That's the point. Good or bad, if you don't put it in your mind, it doesn't exist. If you do then it does. I have learned many things from living among the Maasai, not least from their courage and inner strength. One Japanese volunteer told me 'I am Buddhist and I have practised Zen all my life, but these people, these Maasai, they are Zen.'

It is important, however, that we do not romanticise any culture as our common humanity strives to find itself. Neither should we attach our morals or reality to the things other people do for we all have inside us the twin worlds of kindness and destruction. The human paradox is that these realities often live entwined in each other and heroism lives the same moment as madness. In the furnace of war and hatred, the city of those who love one another is drawn and fused together in the heroism of charity under suffering, while the city of those who hate everything is scattered and dispersed and its citizens are cast out in every direction, like sparks, smoke, and flame. Every moment we have choice. In everything we are, there is the potential to bring joy or sadness – each drawn from the well that is our heart.

Salau was the one of the first Africans I met. It was he who taught me how to say hello although I didn't know it, I thought he was telling me his name. I carefully pointed to myself and said my name, then pointed at him. It had worked in the movies. He looked at the end of my finger as though there were something on it that he should, out of courtesy, inspect. Then he said hello. This isn't as easy as it sounds. Saying hello to the Maasai is a finely nuanced activity. There is a basic hello which the Maasai presume is the most they will elicit from a white person. Actually, it's the adult male hello. There's another for adult female, others for children, and others, more respectful, for male and female elders. And appropriate answers. I was trying to make contact like some latter day Stanley (Me Conroy, You Livingstone, me presume). The reason I was trying to say hello was that Salau was minding goats down at the clinic wearing a loincloth with a businesslike spear. We

Salau had taken off his own cloth and put it on the boy.

had our hopeless two-word conversation and then I drifted away embarrassed while he moved away to something more fulfilling like teaching goats to sing.

Later, I learnt his story. It comes in two halves, one of which was not known while I was hearing the other. Salau and his mother and brother arrived from far south of here. Arrived with nothing. Now, when I say they had nothing you probably think in terms of people whose businesses as recruitment consultants or cell phone entrepreneurs failed and they were left with nothing except a bit of income from their wife's PR practice.

Personal joy is a deception if it does not react and become active in the struggle against hatred, intolerance and prejudice.

Even had to take the children out of ballet. That kind of nothing. Salau and family arrived with the African equivalent. They owned one cloth which Mrs. Salau wore and one gourd in which they carried milk if anyone would give them milk, otherwise water. That was it.

Salau's mother and brother had tuberculosis. The brother was in a bad way and died but the mother was being treated at the clinic though it would be months before she was well. Because Salau was a shepherd, the clinic gave him a job minding the goats. The clinic had goats because they were the standard treatment for malnutrition. If you came across a child with severe malnutrition, you gave the child's mother a goat. For a lot of families, the milk made the difference between serious malnutrition and the sort of malnutrition that counts as a regular Maasai childhood. So the clinic had a herd of goats in case someone turned up with a malnourished child, and therefore needed a goat herd. Salau got a little goat herd's hut and with his first wages he was able to buy himself a cloth to cover himself. Things began to look up.

I was in the vicinity of the clinic one day when I spotted Salau watching over his goats, naked. I went over to see what he was up to and encountered a small boy. The boy was wearing Salau's cloth. I asked Salau who the boy was. 'It's all right', Salau said, 'he's my boy.' But where the boy had come from and who he was took a few days to ascertain – it took that long before the language the boy spoke was identified and someone was found who could speak it.

The boy's story wasn't very heartening. He and his brothers and sisters had been trapped in their family hut which was then set on fire. He didn't know what had happened to his parents but it's safe to assume they were killed by a mob. There were a lot of people massacred during the elections and thousands were made homeless, burned out.

When we are content and sorted in ourselves, there is no need for external affirmation or approval.

He had crouched on the floor of the family hut as it had burned down. The roof had fallen on him and his brothers and sisters. His back was terribly burned but somehow he survived. None of the rest of them did. He set out walking, naked, with his burns weeping and had travelled so far that no one spoke his language when he ran into Salau. Salau had taken off his own cloth and put it on the boy. In his goat herd's hut, the boy slept on the bed and Salau slept on the floor at his feet. The boy shared Salau's food. Salau took the boy out with him every day watching the goats. The boy wore the cloth. Salau was standing there naked when I came along.

There is a sequel to this story. Some months later, Salau sold the whole lot of the clinic's goats and pocketed the money. He was fired though the clinic never got the money back.

We are all light and darkness. But the shadows of our lives should not diminish the light we have cast nor the failures extinguish the victories. In Ronan's story there is a raw heroism, a powerful lesson and a simplicity that needs no interpretation.

Every day there are new stories, more unbelievable accounts of hatred and rage. Each one of us must take part in a collective response to such cruelty, not by shared indignation or sorrow, but by proactively becoming involved in the shaping of events as they occur in our society. Being engaged in the majesty of creation requires more than the personal journey. It demands participation in the journey of humanity itself. Personal joy is a deception if it does not react and become active in the struggle against hatred, intolerance and prejudice. It is not enough to pray for change. It is not enough to applaud the efforts of others. Change requires us all to become aware, become awake, become alive, become dynamically involved in our own families, communities, countries, and planet.

I remember sitting on the veranda of a small cottage in Dodoma in Central Tanzania. I was sprawled on the seat recovering from a long drive. My friend for many years, Job Lusinde, sat beside me and we were chatting. A friend walked in from the garden in the twilight and wandered into the kitchen humming. Job and I continued to share our conversation. A voice from the kitchen asked us whether we were having tea or coffee... a few minutes later how much sugar and milk, then sitting down beside us, Job's friend poured the tea. We sat quietly looking at the sunset together, sharing a few jokes... and gradually it

It takes more courage than we imagine to be perfectly simple with other men.

dawned on me who Job's friend was – Julius Nyerere, one of the great statesmen of the 20th Century. When we are content and sorted in ourselves, there is no need for external affirmation or approval. Anxiety stems from the fear of not being approved of, not being wanted, of being rejected. The confidence of inner joy has no fear because there is nothing to lose.

Image can be distorted by misconceptions and fears. Your idea of me is fabricated with notions you have borrowed from other people and from yourself. What you think of me depends on what you think of yourself. Perhaps you create your idea of me out of material

Of course there's no such thing as a stranger, just someone who hasn't become your friend yet.

that you would like to eliminate from your own idea of yourself. Perhaps your idea of me is a reflection of what other people think of you. Our own self-worth is often linked to how we are seen by others. However, if our happiness is dependent on how others judge us, we are at the mercy of moods and fads, changes and emotions. Self worth should be born from within. It takes more courage than we imagine to be perfectly simple with other men.

False sincerity has much to say because it is afraid. Thomas Merton once wrote :

'There is in every weak, lost and isolated member of the human race an agony of hatred born of his own helplessness, his own isolation. Hatred is the sign and the expression of loneliness, of unworthiness, of insufficiency. And insofar as each one of us is lonely, is unworthy, each one hates himself.'

We often limit ourselves. We have to learn that we are infinite, have unlimited possibility. We have to learn to think outside the concepts and notions of reasoned ideas and reach beyond our horizons. We can be more than who we pretend to be. We are not one thing but many. We are not isolated but together. We are not one colour, we are the whole rainbow.

I was once in a railway station standing behind some schoolgirls who were buying magazines and sweets. One of the teenage magazines had a rather sad looking girl on the front cover and a lead article *'How to lose it before you lose him'* referring to dieting before losing your boyfriend. Another was about concealing your blemishes. The second magazine was 'summer fashion' with a picture of a gorgeous girl sneering at another girl not in fashion. The girl buying these magazines was within the normal weight and height limits for her age but still had a deep anxiety about her appearance. This was further fuelled by her 'friends' joking with her that she was a spotty fat pig. The result of this ongoing amusement was, of course, tears. Some ten minutes later, I noticed the same girl faced into a corner still sobbing her eyes out. I popped into a shop and then went over to the girl and asked her if she was ok. In England, this is rarely done any more because people are afraid to say hello. I put into her hand a small Paddington Bear and a little book of sayings. I cannot remember what the sayings were but I wrote in the first page 'You are great just as you are, and that's the way most people see you.' I signed it from a stranger. Of course there's no such thing as a stranger, just someone who hasn't become your friend yet.

We can all be wounded by the cruel things people can say. I remember in school always being chosen last when playing football. I remember times when I was hurt by people's words. But more than this, I remember one time saying something unkind to a friend and seeing him fall into a flood of tears. I was 16 at the time and as I looked at Johnny's face, looked into his eyes that were pools of hurt, I felt within me a surging emotion that I had not known before. I felt, perhaps for the very first time in my life (but not the last), a sense of shame. I had reduced a friend to tears. This affected me profoundly and something in my heart of hearts

A cynic might say it was the drink, but I would hope it was the humanity that occurs when we see beyond the visible into who people are.

cracked. That crack is still there today reminding me that I once hurt a human being in this world and brought sorrow into their life.

We live in such cynical times, but they will pass. There is too much goodness in the world to be overcome by darkness. If you light a single candle in total darkness, you can see it for miles. If you give a single smile, it's amazing how it spreads. We can do the impossible if we believe in ourselves. When I learned this, I resolved to become the person I had always wanted to be. The other stood there in the corner of my room watching me but I will never let the other into myself again. You don't need feet to dance. Its about what is inside you, about how you see yourself, the rest fits around that.

There is a famous Indian dancer Sudha Chandran, whose amazing charisma and energy gave modern Indian dancing world recognition. People were shattered when she was nearly killed in a car crash. Her legs were smashed and Sudha had to have her right leg amputated. The arts, the creative fires and much of India mourned. Then a year later Sudha Chandran was on stage again, dancing better than ever, amazing audiences with her boundless energy and motion. When interviewed after her first return performance, she laughed and asked 'who ever told you that you need feet to dance?'

So much of the dance is about perceptions. I was meeting some friends in a well-known Dublin hotel. The place was crowded, it was Christmas week, you couldn't breathe for the smoke and the three bars had spilled out into the lobby. I didn't know how I was going to find the guys in this seething mass of humanity.

We Irish are not the most retiring of people, not the shyest once we get going and I had to prise my way through the shoals of socialites. I finally found the main lounge after what seemed a lifetime and saw Tim standing in his designer suit on the piano stool in the corner of the lounge, fag in one hand, brandy in the other waving as if on a life raft, beckoning me in a manner only we can quite get away with. At length I reached them and it was like stepping into a time warp. In this corner of the hotel, all was empty. Half a dozen armchairs and a huge couch were free while the social hoards squashed up against each other like wildebeest crossing the Serengeti in a single body.

Half a dozen armchairs and a huge couch were free while the social hoards squashed up against each other like wildebeest crossing the Serengeti in a single body.

James greeted me in a loud uncontrolled base noise, with a Dublin accent. Mike became 'MOOIEKEEEEEEE' accompanied by a bodily jerk backwards and the facial gymnastics required to release his welcome. You see, James lives in a broken body and his condition has made him somewhat different. He has overcome severe handicap to lecture widely on social human rights and societal illusion.

The reason all the seats around us were empty was because of the inherent discomfort many people feel when they get close to the handicapped or deformed. We spent the evening joking about the dialects of Dublin, Joyce and the things that make us Dubliners. What James lacks in physical ability he makes up for with emotional wisdom and a delicious humour that flows unconsciously. As the evening wore on, those closest to us became less afraid. A cynic might say it was the drink, but I would hope it was the humanity that occurs when we see beyond the visible into who people are.

We are wounded only if we allow ourselves to be, belittled or reduced only if we absorb those things that would reduce us. Remember, no one can make us feel anything without our consent. We are all vulnerable, all easy to wound. Greatness is in those who can make us feel great.

I think that being happy has to start and continue within us all. It's about how I live with my me. The chemistry

I have with myself is reflected in everything else. Who would have thought a poor black girl would end up doing more to change America's values and attitudes than the federal Government. If Oprah Winfrey ran for President, she might just get in. She has single handedly done more for people's rights in America than all the lobbyists in the corridors of power. Why? Because she feels with a passion and she has tapped into the one thing we all share; soul. Oprah Winfrey really believes in herself and in people. But you don't have to be famous to be a role model or to give of the goodness inside you. You don't have to be wealthy to be fulfilled.

Unlike optimists who see the good, often closing their eyes to the bad, truly joyful people embrace reality and merrily get on with doing something about it simply because its natural.

Some time ago we were dealing with a cholera epidemic and a drought, more people dying of AIDS than we could ever cope with and I was charging off to see a donor in the big city.

It was 6am, never my finest hour. As I drove out the gate of our complex I saw a little old lady out the corner of my eye. It was very dry and very hot. There were a dozen people with problems waiting for me on my return and I noticed that the same little old lady I saw in the morning was sitting under a red bougainvillea in the sun. She was talking to the cats, we have many cats. I love cats.

Loidim was very old, had bad eyesight, was barefoot and she could not really see me at all in the sun but I knelt beside her to listen to her problem. She looked up at me with a little surprise in her smile, 'Oh, I don't have a problem. I just thought I would come to help. I know that you are very busy and I thought I would come and help you.' She smiled. She had no teeth. 'I have no money, and I have nothing to give but I do have time, lots and lots of time.' Loidim volunteered with us. Eventually she came to live beside us near our manyatta.

It was only a couple of years later when she died that I learnt the meaning of her name. It means, 'I will do'.

What I suspect is this: there is a common thread running through the lives of those who are happy. There is a sameness in these people who come from every background and situation. I think that we all meet these people in our lives and are all touched by them. Not by anything they do but simply by the way they are themselves. Their attitude is natural and they are often unconscious of it.

I think that kindness, is not about common sense but about a deeper sense – a more lasting and essential sense, a realisation of the things that are the same in us.

Unlike optimists who see the good, often closing their eyes to the bad, truly joyful people embrace reality and merrily get on with doing something about it simply because its natural.

They do not depreciate, judge or pull down. They create, encourage and inspire others. They are not petty as they see the big picture, not just the small print.

Tom Hogan is one of those souls who is incapable of saying anything bad about anyone. He showers fun and humour, energy and pleasure in all directions regardless of whom it hits. He is impervious to cynicism; Tom is the sort who sees well in the devil!

There is a remote mission in the North Eastern desert of Kenya. It's 100°F in the shade, no electricity, high risk, military escort terrain and dangerous with a capital D. It was so violent that everyone had left after endless raids and robberies. Vehicles were hijacked and people hurt. The communities in the desert were destitute and someone had to go and run a relief program. For the last few years Tom had run an extensive child survival, training and disease project then, a few weeks ago, the mission was raided. Tom's version of the story summarised hours of violence and stabbings in the words 'they beat the hell out of us over and over' – which they did. Last week Tom just committed himself to another three years there. He rarely talks about religion or prayer but then again, some people shine so brightly that they don't need to say anything.

Tom is one of the 'Karibu' people. Karibu is a Swahili word of welcome meaning literally 'draw near'. Everything for Tom is 'you're very welcome', 'no problem', 'not a bother'. He treats people as if they are all immediate family and shares the little he has without a thought. Tom and I have a friend called Paul Cunningham. If ever there was a man who delighted in life, it was Paul. He loved everyone and, if there was an incarnation of giving, then he was it. On a bad day, his vocabulary started with terrific, great, fantastic and worked upwards. Paul was over forty years in Africa and we became close friends.

Within them all there is an unspoken realisation, an incommunicable knowledge that does not judge, does not lie down but instead builds, creates and heals.

Just after the Second world War Paul was made chaplain to a Kenyan prison. He had already been in a leper colony in Zanzibar where his magical presence left its mark. As Chaplain, Paul spent a lot of time with prisoners including those who were about to be hung. The condemned were kept apart and Paul's first experience was of a young Maasai Shepherd who had been herding his flock and had wandered onto a farmer's land. The farmer had beaten the boy who defended himself, killing his assailant.

The Maasai was a young warrior and did not understand why he was taken and put in chains and why he was being kept away from the great plains. He did not know what he had done wrong. The young man was very afraid because he had never been caged before. Paul stayed with the Maasai shepherd until the moment of his execution. He was simply present and walked with him. Paul told me something that has stayed in my heart for twenty years.

> *'Sometimes all you can do is be there, be among, be with, listen, smile, hold their hands, sometimes just cry with them, just stay'.*

The young shepherd died, still not knowing why, but his last words as he looked at Paul were Papaiai, which means 'my father', and Paul held his hand until the last second, nearly falling as the trap door shot open. And as Paul said... 'His Father was there to embrace him as he passed into light...'

I learnt so much from his simple delight in enjoying people. He once told me that we choose the direction of our lives every time we open our mouths. In that moment we can choose to heal and forgive, help and bring beginning to others – or not. Paul spoke the language of the heart – he awoke an enthusiasm in everyone, taught them that they were essential. I once asked Paul what he thought the most important thing in the world was. He replied.

'Just love. If we can only learn to forgive, let go of our heads and follow our hearts'. That inner vision is what we have forgotten to trust. In the words of St Augustine:

> *'Facere quod in se, ama et fac quod vis'.*
> *Do what is within you. Love and do what*
> *you like.*

I remember once, in the midst of some crisis, someone saying to Paul 'That guy's a fool. I'm going to give him a piece of my mind!' Paul smiled, took his hand with both of his, looked him straight in the eye and said, 'Give him a piece of your heart instead'... That was Paul's magic; he always saw the big picture.

I once heard Paul preach to a group of prisoners. They ranged from sixteen to forty and there were about a hundred of them. His Swahili was heart Swahili and mine was very bad but I still have a few scribbled notes from what he said some two decades ago. He spoke walking among them, laughing and joking.

> *'We are all prisoners in one way or*
> *another. We are all afraid... we have all*
> *hurt and been hurt... and yes, we have all*
> *been in chains.*
>
> *Lift up each other... do good to those who*
> *hate you... protect the weak among you*
> *and feed the sick first.*

Let's always change our hearts and forgive each other. Forgive yourselves and in time we will learn to see beyond the walls, beyond the chains, maybe even into our hearts and there, if you look carefully enough, you will find a joy you never expected. It's deep inside, I promise you.'

As I looked at Paul, it dawned on me that he really did not see the dirt, the sweltering heat, the chains, the wardens, or the flies. He didn't see criminals. He saw fellow pilgrims.

Paul responded to flattery and abuse the same way – with blissful indifference. He greeted everyone with a hug and a two handed handshake, a joke and a magical charm. His eyes were full of life and excitement, he was always learning and he had a humility that only the wise possess. He could get even the most uptight bureaucrat smiling with his wonderful smile, gentle manner, and pure humanity. His last words to me were 'Mike, I'm off, imagine, all this and Heaven too, see you at home, and remember...' he gave me a big hug, a magical smile and his eyes were full of tears.

'I love you Paul.' I whispered

'I know you do.' he replied.

In every way, Paul was a giver and when he died his earthly possessions filled a pillowcase with room to spare. Paul saw everything as the glory of a Father who delighted in everything. Even when his Alzheimer's became serious, he said to me 'Do you know, it's brilliant because I can read my favourite books and by the time I reach the end I can start again and it is all new. I'm discovering everything over and over again.' Like the Monsignor in Graham Green's Monsignor Quixote, Paul was on a journey of discovery in his last months. The only difference was Paul was laughing and dancing, celebrating and singing, rejoicing and delighting in the magic of it all. Paul's last months were like his life – an example of what life should be, a declaration of joy, a delight in the gift of the present and a song of thanks for everything about us.

The good news is that there are more saints and heroes out there than you could ever imagine.

Our thoughts, our words and our actions are really who we are. When energy leaves you in any way except in strength and trust, it cannot bring back to you anything but pain and discomfort. We were made to release our energy through love and trust. In people like Paul, the fire burns like the Sun. There is a connectedness, a freedom. Because of it, there is really nothing to prove, nothing to learn, nothing to fear because the love is dwelling within and is its own reason.

While the world can undoubtedly be a very mean place, for every feared thing there is an opposing hope that encourages us. All of us have the scars of the insults that have been thrown at us. I have a friend called Tim. He sat beside me in the Pub and told me about his Mum who had just died. Tim, like the rest of us, was knee deep in the usual preoccupations of life. The mortgage, the banks, the stuff that makes up suburban daily life. He had a series of setbacks that would have made most people very bitter. He had been shafted and cheated, maligned and hurt. His innocence had caused him to be taken advantage of and his old style handshake proved a rather unsound business practice. That, coupled with a series of accidents and bad luck, created for Tim often daunting periods in his life.

In the midst of this, he could still be seen making time in his home for, and welcoming, those who brought down the tone of the neighbourhood, visiting strangers in hospital and doing things that to Tim were perfectly normal. Tim is always trying to make a better world. He constantly challenges Ireland's Ministry of Justice which has an Aliens Office that often harasses foreigners trying to process papers. I have seen Tim help complete strangers sort out complex legal problems and I have known him to anonymously put money in strangers' parking meters and go shopping for people who are sick.

When I fly into Ireland for increasingly brief trips, Tim does all he can to help. He does so with humour and delight, and when other friends might tell me to get stuffed, he has never once said no. We have campaigned together, often fruitlessly, but unfazed soldiered on. I can lift the phone and ask Tim to help people he has never heard of or I might ask him to do some next to impossible task and, whether he achieves it or not, he really does take one serious run at it and gives it everything he has. I have never heard Tim say a bad word against anybody. Come to that I cannot remember ever seeing Tim angry though, I for one, have often given him good reason to be. It's always the way with people like Tim that the best stories cannot be written down.

I do remember though the man dying of AIDS, and rejected by many in his own family, who was embraced by Tim and always in his home. The people that discouraged his kindness as imprudent. I think that kindness, is not about common sense but about a deeper sense – a more lasting and essential sense, a realisation of the things that are the same in us. I think that one day, perhaps, all men might learn this sense that we are one, this state of being. Kindness is not measured because its nature is unconditional. It permeates all around us and gives because of itself. Kindness emanates its own delight, its own joy – it is not thought out in the head but lived out in what we do. Kindness, like all joy is magnetic, contagious. We are drawn to those who love and cherish, those who make us whole. Kindness can make people rethink their lives.

On one of Tim's many trips to Africa, I found him laughing and joking with a group of very old women. Neither Tim nor the women understood anything that was going on but he managed to find out they were from a village destroyed by drought and he went to visit them. Typical Tim. He got sunburn returning without sunglasses, hat, shirt and bag, all of which had been given away en route.

Another morning, Tim had managed to get his hands on an egg. This egg he proudly boiled and it was to be his breakfast on safari. Of course he never ate it. If a friend is someone who stands by you, is always there for you, is always quietly at your side, utterly present, then Tim gives new honour to the name friend.

The threads that connect the lives of the people in this chapter are that they all have the spirit of the child within them. Within them all there is an unspoken realisation, an incommunicable knowledge that does not judge, does not lie down but instead builds, creates and heals. It is positive and indomitable and, above all, it is connected to something that we desperately lack. All of us have met people who in one way or another inspire, enrich or stand apart from everyone else. We need in our lives those who call us to be aware, to be awakened.

There are plenty of critics telling us what is wrong. The good news is that there are more saints and heroes out there than you could ever imagine. When we get distracted by the anguish and misery in the world, we can forget that we are surrounded by majesty and greatness and unbelievable goodness and self-sacrifice. Some people, God puts his arm around them. Like all good news, however, it's rarely told.

The celebration of life entails us letting go of fear, freeing ourselves from the anxieties that keep us from living our dreams. We must trust the child within us, never giving up, gripping life with both hands and leaping into the full tide of everything before us. In order to really enjoy the passion of life, we must break the unconscious patterns that create these familiar negative cycles of thoughts and action. We need to be free of fear and stress. Only then will we be surprised by joy.

As we walk through life we encounter people who drain us, others who leave us indifferent but there are also those, every now and then, who uplift us; those who, through their own energy, inspire and awaken us. The people who inspire me invariably have a boundless sense of fun, a childlike enthusiasm and with it a delicious sense of adventure and discovery. Because they delight in everything they have no anxiety. People can succeed at almost anything when they have enough enthusiasm. The future belongs to those who believe in the beauty of their dreams. The future belongs to you even as you decide now to live them. Magic is all about us. It fills the fabric of creation. The dance can fill our lives if we take the time to see it. The laughter of a child, an unspoken connection with a stranger, moments of harmony with nature. In everything there is the call to become, to belong, and the promise of light.

Magic is all about us. It fills the fabric of creation.

Secrets Of Joy

'Throughout the whole of life one must continue to learn to live. The same stream of life that runs through the world runs through my veins night and day in rhythmic measure. It is the same life that shoots in joy through the dust of the earth into numberless waves of flowers.'

Rabindranath Tagore

Like all great mysteries, the secrets of inner joy are very simple. They thrive all around us and are, as with everything that really matters, within our grasp. The dance we spoke of is simply the living of a happy life, a life full of love. Some people are so connected to the stream of life that Rabindranath Tagore speaks of that they exude not just happiness but energy.

For us all, every thought, every word, every interaction is energy. Each time we laugh, cry, watch television, go shopping – in everything we do there is an energy given and absorbed. A happy life requires positive energy, solution focused thinking and a big 'yes' approach. It also requires a lot of giving. Not simply giving to others but giving, in a new way, to ourselves by reclaiming space, making time, creating positive experiences. Just by being kind to ourselves. In our can do, must work, rush by society, this kind of self-caring is not instilled in us.

☾ ☾ ☾

There was a Monastery where the ancient sages studied. The wisdom of the Zen masters was kept there. The great library contained ten thousand scrolls; the ancient texts of Tao, of Confucius, of the dawn of Zen. Everything was there – from the teachings of prophets and mystics to the books of the dead and the scrolls of time.

In the inner sanctum were kept the books known only by the greatest gurus and prophets. In the first rooms, the books were written on ivory in Sanskrit texts – these held the secrets of enlightenment. They shared the secrets of history, the paths of the ancients, the ways of men and the mysteries of life. They were the books of mystics.

Behind great silver doors were kept the holy books that held the secrets of magic. These were written on sheets of silver, in words that could be seen only by those whose hearts were pure. These books held the secrets of the ages and revealed the ways of wonder, incantations and spells, magical beasts. These were the books of wizards.

Behind three golden gates there was a golden chamber. At the centre of this magnificent room stood a great shrine and, within the shrine, a splendid altar upon which was the most perfect golden image of the Buddha. Lying beneath the feet of Buddha was a small scroll made of white gold. Upon this scroll was written the secret of wisdom. It possessed the answers to all questions and it was the secret of secrets – it was the way of letting go and freeing the heart. The secrets were written in the tears of Buddha. This was the book of Saints.

Only the great Lama himself ever entered this chamber though he had never touched the sacred scroll. Beyond this chamber there was a door but it was a door made entirely of love. Through this door was the book of life and its words were the laughter of children and the songs of birds. It was written in joy and could be read only by passing through the door of love as a child.

The sages and prophets did not believe in the legend. Few believed in the invisible room. Only the great Lama knew its secret for he had played there as a child. Only he knew the name of the room and where it was. It was the heart of God and it was within all men.

If we are going to live love in our actions, we need to be aware of self-deception and be conscious of the difference between talking about love and loving. For myself, there was a time when I spoke about the poor, felt for them, wrote about them, but that was a lot easier than actually going and living with the people who struggled for survival. The idea that the poor are some innocent, repressed group all united in a common struggle is as real as the belief that they share a common goal. They have as many opinions and divisions as anyone else. In fact the 'they' does not exist any more than 'we' as a collective exists. Love might be blind but it is not stupid. Love is awake. Awake to needs, fears and tenderness. But love is not as fickle or variable as our emotions.

There are many types and expressions of love. The intimacy I share with a lover is other than the tenderness I have for my Mother or the chemistry I have with a close friend. The touch I give in sexual union has a different energy to the embrace I give a stranger, each valid in itself. All these expressions spring from my discovery of new synergies and dynamics as I reveal myself.

Balancing these energies of love is as essential as is the realisation that the centre of these is giving without conditions, giving because of itself. We make our living by what we get. We make a life by what we give.

☾ ☾ ☾

My heart tells me that there is a spark that belongs to us all and that, in some way, we are part of each other yet, like love and wonder, we cannot put it into words. We share so many common experiences – taste, pleasure, excitement, fear, laughter... and yet we understand so little of ourselves. As we look

The future belongs to those who believe in the beauty of their dreams.

around us we are faced with contradictions and paradoxes. We are faced with unanswerable questions.

The horrors of poverty and the unkindness around us 'cannot be reasoned away, excused, or papered over with platitudes'. It is not enough to appeal to a God who allows such suffering. Nor is it enough to blame the apathy of men or deceit of politicians. So we are faced with more questions than answers in our struggle to find ourselves. It is easy to become skeptical and cynical in such a world.

In making sense of the absurd, it is important that we do not replace our critical faculties and capacity for scepticism with a spirituality that is blind to the contradictions and pain around us. We need to find that perennial, indomitable 'yes' to life and the only place it dwells is in

Through this door was the book of life and its words were the laughter of children and the songs of birds.

our inner child, in our innocence. Winston Churchill gave many famous speeches in his life. The man who rallied Europe in the face of war was asked to address Oxford University with its hushed assembly of Dons and students, the rich and the powerful, the aspiring and those who were beginning their road of discovery. Churchill uttered only three words to them...

He looked at them with all the fire and passion and determination of a man who had done the impossible. His unbroken spirit had more than once lifted a nation. Now an old man but still undaunted, indomitable, his voice boomed out echoing through the ancient auditorium and he shook the dust of the chancelled eaves... He spoke again...

'NEVER GIVE UP!'

He then left the podium and, for minutes, the silenced crowd were rooted. The standing ovation carried on even as Churchill's car passed through the gates of Oxford London bound.

Oprah Winfrey said:

*'When I look into the future, it's so
bright it burns my eyes'.*

I think this is true. The most fabulous things are happening
all over the world. There are more people doing more good
in more voluntary organisations around the world than
there are soldiers. There are more human beings alive than
ever before. We have never
mixed as much, shared as
much or communicated as
much as we do now. There are
less dictators now than ever

*We make our living by what
we get. We make a life by what
we give.*

before and countries around the world are waking up to the
possibilities of a fairer world. Great things are happening.
The bigots and sores of intolerance are being met with more
and more opposition. Everywhere people are standing up and
trying to do something. For every angry rap song there is a
beautiful expression about love.

☾ ☾ ☾

There is often no sense to or explanation for real life.
All we can do is decide how we will live, what we
will do. We respond to the world around us in many ways.

We rarely follow a single ideology and those who profess a common doctrine have a thousand interpretations of it. We relate to reality with often shifting perceptions, values and emotions.

As we walk uncertainly through this world, the deepest longing within us all is surely to be loved, to be safe. I suspect that we hope to be loved completely. Not to be loved for whom we are, not to be loved for what we are, not to be loved for what we might become, but to be loved. To be utterly cherished, wanted, accepted just as we are. To be unconditionally loved.

If you have ever been in love, you know what it's like to be totally crazy. The outside world cannot touch you; nothing can get you down or hurt you. You are possessed, drowned, blinded by the passion and joy and ecstasy of being in love. It is an all-consuming fire that transforms you and makes every ordinary thing wonderful and exciting. It is a transformation of everything, a reality change. Being in love, you wonder how you drew breath before you met the person you are in love with. You channel the most extraordinary energy into the relationship finding oceans of feeling and power, a discovery of a different you. Here lies the secret, it is not really a different you – it's the real you.

There are more people doing more good in more voluntary organisations around the world than there are soldiers.

☾ ☾ ☾

In our work in Africa, we spend a lot of our time caring for people who are dying of AIDS and a lot of our projects try to create ways of responding to people living in extreme poverty. Every morning when I wake up, I am greeted by a young Kenyan called Elle. Elle is probably the closest most of us will get to meeting an angel this side of heaven. Since he was a child, he beamed out at the world through the most magical of smiles. Elle is one of those rare beings whose greatest pleasure is to give. He is, in a near mystical way, full of raw undiluted happiness.

Despite the often tragic nature of our work, Elle's spirit is so full of harmony that I have never seen him drained or low. It is not a Buddhist's tranquillity of detachment or a serenity born of disengagement. It is more wonderful than that. It is a natural delight, the pleasure of just being, an innate joy

That all joy comes from selflessness and lasting happiness comes from kindness.

fuelled by the energy of profound calm that lives in the midst of human need and poverty. Joy is the infallible sign of the presence of God.

☾ ☾ ☾

We are a part of a real mystery, and even though we can't see what is happening, we can sense that we share in it's unfolding. The more I travel, the more people I meet, the more I realise that we are one. Within each of us lies infinite possibility drawn from the same source that caused the universe into being. We are not only valuable – we are essential. We were called to become pure love. But where does all this love and positive energy fit into the torn world we live in. Where is the relevance of these secrets to the real world and how do these reflections measure up when confronted with life?

We need to find that perennial, indomitable 'yes' to life and the only place it dwells is in our inner child, in our innocence.

When asked about cruelty Gandhi replied:

> *'When I despair, I remember that all through history truth and love have always won. There have been tyrants, and murderers, and for a time they can seem invincible, but in the end they always fall. Think of it... always.'*

$$\mathbb{C} \quad \mathbb{C} \quad \mathbb{C}$$

As I write, we are in the midst of a drought in Africa. Under trees I see infants trying to feed from mothers whose frail bodies try to protect their children from the searing sun and young men, too weak to walk, waiting for death in the shade. Others in camps, in long lines, are waiting for food that has been delayed until the TV cameras arrive.

Across the world today there are millions of people in jails and prisons, many being tortured. There are all kinds of abuse from interrogation to the debasement and humiliation of prisoners at the hands of wardens as they fall into the habit of treating inmates like animals. In much of the world, little is done to protect prisoners. I have visited prisons in many parts of Africa where inmates exist in unspeakable conditions,

We are a part of a real mystery, and even though we can't see what is happening, we can sense that we share in it's unfolding.

enduring degradation and violence. This is especially so with young prisoners, some of whom may only be detained, uncharged, and finally released.

There was a boy. We will call him 'Blesse'. He was twenty-two and when I first saw him he was covered in blood. He had stabbed himself three times in the stomach. Blesse had been detained for three weeks at a city jail before finally being released without charge. He had only been held as he had no identification on him as he was walking home. That was his crime but a few hours later, without even returning to his home, he found a sharp piece of glass and tried to kill himself behind the Cathedral.

Like many young men in prisons around the world, Blesse was a sexual opportunity for the inmates. Having resisted initially, he was repeatedly raped and used for the weeks he was detained. No attempt to help him was made. His very badly damaged body could be repaired but the fear and horror, anguish and humiliation were far worse as they had destroyed everything Blesse ever was. His teeth had been carefully removed so he could be used in other ways by two rapists at a time. His body was covered in the welts of a whip and the weals of a cane, his wrists are still scarred from embedded chains.

Blesse contracted HIV as well as a number of other infections, but in time his wounds were healed and he could walk again. But his life had been brutally crushed. It was only with time and gentleness and a lot of sharing that the emotional trauma and bile began to ease. Blesse now works in central Africa as an AIDS and rape crisis counsellor and is happily married. He is married to one of the nurses who cared for him on the night the glass shard was removed from his stomach.

☾ ☾ ☾

'There are two things which men can do
about the pain of disunion with other
men. They can hate or they can love.
Hatred recoils from the sacrifice and the
sorrow that are the price of this resetting
of bones. It refuses the pain of reunion.'
Merton New Seeds of Contemplation

I am only a man but my response to the reality in front of me cannot be abdicated. It is by taking my own joy into the world around me that I can bring joy. I can cry and complain but that will help no one, or I can try and do something. Whatever the something is, it should not eclipse my inner light or my own energy because then I would burn out or become a pain in the neck, obsessed with wrong, rather than focused on what can be done. In this sharing of our inner selves, we discover that the greatness within us has no horizons. My being becomes being in love. It is the centre of everything as long as it lasts.

'From it flows one's desires and fears,
one's joys and sorrows, one's discernment
of values, one's decisions and deeds'.

This is why we are alive – to discover and live this kind of love. All of us need to be loved and we need to love.

☾ ☾ ☾

This then is the secret. That all joy comes from selflessness and lasting happiness comes from kindness. The secret of living a life full of joy is to weave the threads of goodness through our daily lives. Where you do not find love, put love – and then you will find love. It is impossible to generate calm in others unless you are still in yourself. So too, without an internal spring of energy, you cannot pour out energy. You can only pretend to. Ultimately, if you want *others* to be happy, practice compassion. If *you* want to be happy, practice compassion. In all things we are transformed by our compassion because compassion is not conscious acts but a way of life.

That all joy comes from selflessness and lasting happiness comes from kindness.

Joy is a recognition of the beauty and mystery all around us. It is being awakened and surprised by the countless gifts we are given every day. It is seeing kindness and friendship, goodness and caring for 'it is only with the heart that one sees rightly'. Inner joy breathes forgiveness. It lets go of everything that drains us. It gets rid of limits and allows us to see ourselves as limitless.

BECOMING

*'He to whom this emotion is a stranger, who can
no longer pause to wonder and stand rapt in
awe, is as good as dead: his eyes are closed.'*

Einstein

In all our lives, no matter what our commitments and obligations, we need time to step back a little and, in taking such moments, step out of time, step away from ourselves and let go of ourselves long enough to taste that wonder and energy that binds us. This space gives us back to ourselves, takes us back to our origin and source. In this space silence speaks.

One cold wet morning I was sitting in the chancelled eve of a transept in Chartres cathedral. The silent majesty of Chartres reaches back through the corridors of history to the sacred glades where the Druids communed with the universe in mystical rites long forgotten. For centuries, their most sacred place was here where Caesar slaughtered the last resistance to Rome and raised a temple to Mars in a glade ancient even in those times. Here Augustus placed an alter to Aphrodite. It was at Chartres that the shrine to Antinous, beloved of Hadrian, was built and here that the cult of Antinous rivalled Christianity for a hundred years with the resurrected Antinous offering perfection and new life. Chartres radiates a spiritual vitality, a calm disinterest in the passage of the centuries and the changing beliefs of generations.

I was lost in the boundless space that comes when we let go of our thoughts and distractions and give way to the fullness of stillness – a crystal, active, stillness full of energy. It was then I opened my eyes. I had not even raised my head. Everything around me was transformed by light. The profusion of colour surged around me and the depth of the light filled the shadows. The rays of the sun penetrated through the magnificent stained glass, striking shafts of colour throughout the cloistered chapels and tombs in a silent luminescence. Everything about me lay bathed, entrapped in beams of red and purple, mantled in symphonic colour. The plain chant I had come to sing began:

"And it is thee alone who holds up the stars, thee alone who calls the universe into being, thee alone who is forever one - it is thee who is about us".

We live with an invisible sun inside us. But in order to become light we must evolve, change, grow. To become, we need to be in touch with the energy within all creation. We need to be open to wonder, aware of things greater than ourselves. The Dalai Lama, in writing of the modern world, repeats several times his sense that people have unnecessarily divided themselves. He has come to the conclusion 'that whether or not a person is a religious believer or not does not matter much. Far more important is that they be a good human being. We humans can live quite well without recourse to religious faith'. But he then goes on to separate the creeds and doctrines of faiths from spirituality which is about the things of the human spirit 'such as love and compassion, patience, tolerance, forgiveness, contentment, a sense of responsibility, a sense of harmony'. The Dalai Lama explains that while we can do without religion, 'what we cannot do without are these basic spiritual qualities'. We often think of ourselves in a physical sense, forgetting that we are primarily energy. We can transform our self-understanding. We are intelligent beings searching for reason in a world where there is much suffering and loneliness and pain. We look out at the contradictions around us and realise that we are not only rational, but emotional also. We are vulnerable and easily hurt, we laugh and cry and doubt and imagine... we are spiritual beings as well.

We often assume that our next breath is there, that the next week will be along as usual. Until something happens that shifts the world from under us and our expectations shatter... an accident, an illness, a death. When you see the face of death – in yourself or someone you love – you are rarely ever the same again. There is often a reality check so profound that all the things we fuss over and worry about get thrown out of the window. I remember one day feeling somewhat self absorbed. Among the people waiting to see me when I returned was a fragile, dazed looking woman and her two children. The woman wanted help...

She told her story with a detachment I had seen before. Her voice was calm, matter of fact and held no emotion. She had five children. Her eldest son had been crucified along with his classmates and then burnt alive, her eldest daughter raped and her body nailed to the wall of their hut. She did not know what had happened to her husband who was a school teacher in a small town but most of the people in her village had been set on fire or macheted to death. She escaped but her 14-year-old son had keloid scars across a back completely disfigured from being whipped with barbed wire.

I left the room to vomit, and when I returned I noticed my walkman was missing off my desk and smiled to myself at my noticing. It is not enough to tell you that, even now, I cry remembering the presence of this family. It is not enough to tell you of the raging anger of those who were there or the trembling or the unspeakable emotion. Not enough to describe the body of the boy or their eyes that had witnessed things that are outside the scope of the most perverted imagining. It is not enough to merely help, merely react, merely to do something. When we as human beings do not learn within our interiority, within our personal lives, from this then we are, in some part, dying.

There is such a thing as evil, and it's alive and well. Not in some remote demon or satanic cult but in the fabric and mores of ordinary life, in the essential mechanics of global economics and injustice. But there is also an evil that lives in men. A prejudice, a blindness that comes, often imperceptibly, into our lives. And there is hate, a hate

> *'That takes joy in hating. It is strong*
> *because it does not believe itself to be*
> *unworthy and alone. It feels the support*
> *of a justifying God.'*
> Merton

Every day that we watch the news we can see examples of that hatred.

Nothing has changed in the history of the world. The good are lied about, the beautiful scarred by men and the innocent struck down. Goodness is dismembered, selfishness put on thrones and lust rewarded with gifts. This rage within men creates petty hatreds and divisions and the wounds that tear men from union with one another widen and open into wars. Love is massacred in each act of anger. Light is murdered in each act of unkindness. I think that in the face of inhumanity, raging madness and cynicism, the victory of the human spirit is in the hope that emerges from the ruins of innocence.

Tenderness, decency, raw human goodness, treating people with some sense that they are of us, that they are ours, restoring some shred of life – I think that brokenness begins to heal somewhere from this. One can see the faint emergence of a new beginning in parts of Rwanda, for example. Nevertheless, there are still real arteries of hatred waiting in the shadows, muzzled, ravenous, cowering, but still there. Our lives begin to end the day we become silent about things that matter. The

In order to become light we must evolve, change, grow.

world is tired of anger and cynicism, the politics of personal destruction and a media that sells itself through stories of scandals, failures and tragedies. Although that is undoubtedly part of what is happening, what we do not hear about are the acts of goodness, the deeds of greatness, the struggle to heal in the world. Never forget...

We are magic, we are power, we are promise.

In the story of the Young King, Oscar Wilde tells of a shepherd who had been chosen by God to be king. He saw through the power of men and the wealth of churches and saw how far they had come from the word of God. And the Bishop said 'The burden of this world is too great for one man to bear, and the world's sorrow too heavy for one heart to suffer.' 'Sayest thou that in this house?' said the young King and he strode past the Bishop, climbed up the steps of the altar and stood before the image of Christ. He stood before the image of Christ, and on his right hand and on his left hand were the marvellous vessels of gold, the chalice with yellow wine, and the vial with the holy oil. The great candles burned brightly by the jewelled shrine and the smoke of the incense curled in thin blue wreaths through the dome. He bowed his head in prayer and the priests in their stiff copes crept away from the altar.

Suddenly a wild tumult could be heard in the street outside and in entered the nobles with drawn swords and nodding plumes and shields of polished steel. 'Where is this dreamer of dreams?' they cried. 'Where is this King who is apparelled like a beggar – this boy who brings shame upon our state? Surely we will slay him for he is unworthy to rule over us.' And the young King bowed his head again and prayed, and when he had finished his prayer, he rose up and turning round, he looked at them sadly.

We are intelligent beings searching for reason in a world where there is much suffering and loneliness and pain.

And lo! Through the painted windows came the sunlight streaming upon him and sunbeams wove round him a tissued robe that was fairer than the robe that had been fashioned for his pleasure. The dead staff blossomed and bore lilies that were whiter than pearls. The dry thorn blossomed and bore roses that were redder than rubies. Whiter than fine pearls were the lilies and their stems were of bright silver. Redder than male rubies were the roses and their leaves were of beaten gold. And the people fell upon their knees in awe and the nobles sheathed their swords and did homage, and the Bishop's face grew pale, and his hands trembled. 'A greater than I hath crowned thee,' he cried, and he knelt before him. And the young King came down from the high altar and passed home through the midst of the people. But no man dared look upon his face for it was like the face of an angel.

In every moment of our lives there is that same wonder, the same mystery that crowned the young king. The same inexplicable majesty of creation singing and dancing around us, within us, about us. In every breath there is a miracle. In every voice, in every touch, tear, smile. This wonder has many names. This becoming is known to all faiths for it is the path of enlightenment, the way of compassion and the emptying of the self. It is the coming of joy and the presence of love in our everything. To love is to discover in others the spark of spirit. It is a spirit not owned by creeds or groups. It has many faces – Gandhi and Tutu, Martin Luther King and Mandela, Brownowski and Chardin – icons that touch our souls and remind us of what we could become. It is the spirit of Love and it has many names and still more witnesses for many candles can be kindled from one candle without diminishing its flame. Spiritual awakening is the most essential thing in man's life and it is the sole purpose of being. Perhaps every one of us fellow travellers can remind each other, making our lives a place of healing and becoming, adventure and dynamic discovery. Today lived fully makes every yesterday an example for tomorrow and sows the seeds of change.

'I promise to oppose bravely all that is stupid and bigoted and cruel. Toleration is the highest virtue, humility comes next. Our bones may moulder and become the earth of the fields but the spirit issues forth and lives on high in brightness and mystery and delight. God is the common Father of all mankind'.
Confucious

There is no life beyond redemption, no failure that is beyond recovery, no suffering that cannot be healed and no human being unworthy of our love. There is nothing you can do that will diminish the love and power of Gods grace. You are his child and your name is carved into the palm of his hand and you are everlasting. You are beautiful and you are perfect because you were made by the origin of all things and you were made that he could love you and delight in your love of all creation.

There was once a woman I met in a housing support project who had been so badly beaten by her husband that she had lost her baby and as a result of her injuries she was advised that she could not have children again. Janet was one of many women in protective housing which remains under-funded in England. Janet told me that her daughter, who was with her, had watched as she was dragged to the kitchen by her hair, kicked in the stomach and her face pressed into the dog food. Why was she treated like this? Because she had not cooked for her husband.

As is the case with most domestic violence, the cyclic behaviour of violence, emotional, verbal or physical, creates its own hypnotic dependency making it incredibly hard to get out. Janet succeeded. She went to university, got her own place, is now in a healthy loving relationship and works in the housing support project helping other abused women to get their lives back. How did Janet get out?

By just listening to those voices early on, those gut instincts, that intuition, always trust that primal instinct, it's very rarely wrong. Usually other people around you see it and tell you to get out before you spot it, but like most people I was in denial. How could I be so wrong, how could I build my life for it to get this bad, so we just lived in total denial.

*You can't get out until you realise just
how far gone your own sense of reality
has become'.*

In most human situations it's the same story – we just go along with things, live with cycles of behaviour and patterns of habit. Sometimes it is easier to live with the anguish than face the alternative.

We need to realise what is within us. What is driving us, draining us, lifting us and distracting us. We need to give ourselves enough personal solitude to allow us to discern the emotional and human imperatives that make us unique and special. It is within this reflection that we become awake. It is in becoming awake that we can become conscious of other dimensions and meaning within our lives and it is through this awareness that we begin to become.

The way we deal with the world is a mirror of how we deal with our daily lives. The way we deal with our daily lives is determined by how we love ourselves. This is where all journeys begin – in our deepest selves. We have spoken of the many ways we can look for direction and the countless pressures that can distract us from becoming who we truly are. We have shared examples of ordinary people who dance into the lives of those around them. We have learnt the simple truth that life is a pure flame and that, if it is nurtured, we can set fire to the whole world. So when we perceive the pure, the true, the Holy, the sacred by whatever name, what do we do then? When you finish this book, you may ask what within my heart has changed, what within my deepest self has been touched, what can become from this?

The answer is as simple as the question. We can, wherever possible, as often as possible, commit acts of simple goodness, infect others with tenderness, breathe gentleness, be kind in every direction, be patient when there is no reason to be patient. These are the ways in which we can change the world around us. 'The guidance we need for this cannot be found in science and technology, but it can still be found in the traditional wisdom of mankind.' These are the last words of Schumachers 'Small is Beautiful' which examines the current obsession with profit and progress. We have

Spiritual awakening is the most essential thing in man's life and it is the sole purpose of being.

yet to learn that being rich is not about money or how much stuff we collect, but about our capacity for enjoyment and love. We can spend our lives trying to figure out what to do or we can just start.

With love there are no rules. There are a million little things we can do all the time that will touch people around us – our smile, our warmth, our passion, our joy, our whole way of being. It does not matter where we start, only that we generate love. The evil in this world is not just because evil men do evil things but that good men do nothing. It might be visiting a lonely neighbour, visiting the local prison, paying for the person behind you at a tollbooth, doing something anonymously for a stranger. It really does not matter very much who or why. We suffer when we feel we are giving more than we receive but giving is the door to free ourselves from ourselves. We begin by imagining that we are giving to others, we end by realising that they have enriched us. The Dalai Lama put it like this.

'This is my simple religion. There is no need for temples, no need for complicated philosophy. Our own brain, our own heart is our temple; the philosophy is kindness.'

Through the years, there have been many times that I have been with children who are very sick or who are dying. The great majority of them die simply because there is not enough food for them in the world or enough water. Over many months they become weak and wasted, eventually becoming those living skeletons that turn into dead statistics. There are often people who have gone too far down the path of no return, many who cannot be pulled back from the massive damage of starvation and repeated disease. These are the ones who make up those numbers we see on CNN... you know the ones in the international news segment. 'Thirty thousand die in the Sudan according to the UN, ten thousand in some other country we never heard of, rebels steal food'... hmm, no helping some people.

I have never liked statistics very much. They never set fire to hearts. But the stats are actually people, people with children who once giggled and played with their little brother and hopped and skipped and made little sand castles and played ball and had a favourite toy and hugged their mum and kissed her goodnight.

Recently there was a little girl whose mother had died of dehydration and starvation. She was the last of the family to collapse and despite the best efforts of her mum to save her, Tama was in her last hours, unable even to shut her eyes, covered in flies, the familiar smell of death accentuated by the searing heat of the night.

She laid her head on my lap and her breath grew laboured.

'I am afraid, I can't see.'

'Don't be afraid.'

'Are you there? Hold my hand.'

'The pain will go away, won't it?'

'Soon little one, soon there will be no pain, its ok.'

'Will I be alone.'

'Not alone angel, next time you open your eyes your Mum will be here instead of me and you will be home.'

'And I will play again.'

She was tired and her words almost inaudible. She was very weak and her breath was long and shallow.

'Will you come and play too?'

'Soon angel, soon, yes, I promise, I'll come and play too...'

'Sleep, sweetness, go to sleep now.' I whispered.

And the little one fell asleep and awoke in a kinder world, in a fairer world. And I will keep my promise. Some day I shall play with her.

I cannot tell you what it is like to be a mother knowing you cannot feed your child but I have sat with many who tell me it is a hell without light, a horror seeing the ones you would give your life for starve in front of you. Some say the nights are the worst – cuddling up to children who cannot sleep for the pain they are in.

Spiritual awakening is the most essential thing in man's life and it is the sole purpose of being.

Others say the day, watching the slow disintegration of their infants. I was sitting recently talking to a mother who was caring for her daughter who is very sick and she told me that the biggest change in her life was being able to share her fears and anger, depression and sense of failure, even her thoughts of self-hatred, with others and discovering that these reactions were not some sin on her soul but were part of the stressful process she and others were going through. So too, we all need to feel a sense of support, a sense that there is someone out there who knows what we are going through.

Let's imagine for a moment a little girl, let's call her Mary, is found in a rubbish site in our home area. The girl is nine years old and almost blind from neglect. Her hair has fallen out and her joints pain her. The little girl had not eaten a full meal in months and she is so weak she cannot walk. Mary's face is like an old woman's – wrinkled and sunken – her tiny body is grossly underweight. Her legs are covered in marks like bruises and with peeling sores. Her tongue is red and sore and there are ulcers. The hospital puts her in intensive care and the journalists give her story front page coverage. Every soul in our town is enraged, every parents blood boils. If Mary was in our neighbourhood, it would rightly cause an outrage and her recovery would become everyone's concern. The hospital would be flooded with gifts and visitors. The outpouring of help would have journalists congratulating us on our response. Our own countries do have cases of neglect and abuse, in fact, the numbers of children in need rise every year. But Mary was never neglected by her parents. She was loved and cherished as just the most wonderful thing in their lives. Mary is one of many children who live not so far away from us but not quite close enough. Can you imagine the children you know not being fed to the point they are almost about to die before someone helps them? It leaves very real damage within.

Part of our work is turning the tide a little. Creating answers and solutions through indigenous cultures and traditions, not through our Western ideas, so that change can happen in the real world that others inhabit. While it is true that there are thousands of children who do die of starvation, there are also hundreds of thousands who are dragged back from the precipice of death and a majority of those live full lives. It is true there is mindless violence across our country but for every violent man, there are a hundred gentle men and for every broken home, there are many loving homes. It is true that there is profound corruption destroying nations, but never before have so many publicly fought against it.

There are great achievements happening every day. There is hope and there's a lot of it around. Everywhere we look we will find examples of extraordinary courage and heroism, selflessness and kindness. People don't have to be holy or great or saints, they just have to be human. Our heroes are as flawed and weak as we are – they have bad moods, headaches, they can argue and complain, lie and let you down sometimes, but it does not mean that there is not greatness within them. In life, we can choose to be victims or lovers, we can write our own script.

One of the most magical and amazing feelings you can ever experience is at the moment a severely malnourished child no longer hangs a drawn grey skull, like a corpse. No longer shows teeth in a dry open mouth, solemn and helpless. If we can rehydrate this child, help her mother to feed her, release her from the grip of hunger, there will come a moment... She will turn her head to you on her own, she will open her eyes, and she will smile. There are no words to tell you what that feels like. If you have ever seen your own child step over into a place where you can not help her or reach her in her suffering, and then step back again into life with you, then that is some glimmer. The torment of a parent watching the destruction of their little angel slowly each day has no earthly equivalent, nor has the delight of seeing a child start to feed again, smile again, laugh again. What does it cost to turn a life around...? Sometimes less than buying a CD or a Pizza. Life is a balance between giving and receiving. We do not have to become destitute to help others. We can enjoy our lives and share as well.

Among the many visitors who come to Africa and see our projects was an elderly couple. As usual, one of our field teams brought Billy and Lynne down into the interior and showed them a disease control project operated by grandmothers. Granny power is at the heart of a lot of our success. We thought no more about the visit; it was one among hundreds of such day trips and we were delighted with their company. Billy and Lynne were energetic, caring and kind but little prepared us for what was to come. In response to the villages they had seen, the courage of the mothers fighting overwhelming poverty and disease, Billy and Lynne quietly went back to Canada.

Lynne cares for the terminally ill. After a successful career as an accountant, she decided to go back to college and become a nurse to keep her daughters' company. They drew together their network of family and friends, established ICROSS in Canada and in the first twelve months had sent over three tons of essential medical supplies to Africa. In the process they touched the lives of many people who were searching for ways to do something concrete and effective. People wanted a way to personally make a difference. There are many heroes all around us; mostly they quietly touch the lives of others. If we watched CNN less and looked around more, we would see the real news going on and a lot of it is great news. There are many people giving of themselves in amazing ways all the time. There is a bedridden boy who made us a web site to share our work. There are two old sisters who live in Dublin's inner city who send us three pounds of their old age pension every month. I am often overwhelmed by the sheer tide of goodness and courage I see all around me. I am inspired every day by the countless little acts of anonymous self sacrifice and caring. All about us is the dance – we have only to look up and we shall see it. All about you, and within you, there is goodness, promise, grace and boundless love.

We have been exploring goodness, humanity, the joy

of being fully alive. Trying to figure out where love and gentleness can be in a world full of contradiction, stress, madness and pressure. 'Everywhere people ask, 'what can I actually do'? There are a thousand real ways we can act, create, construct and build. The poor, the suffering, the needy around me, wherever I am, is not someone else's problem. The buck stops here. True I can't be all things to all men, but I can start by being a giver, a carer, a lover to those around me and finding out how I can make a real difference. Taking responsibility means recognising that there is a solution. You are the solution. It is beyond analysis, beyond understanding. Long ago it was said 'You shall be asked. What have you done with all the time that was given to you? How have you used it?'

If we begin by being surprised every morning at everything around us we begin to see the newness in everything. We discover passion and renewal and the energy of nature throbbing and showing us new dimensions of everything we take for granted. The wonder and fun and enthralment that gets lost in adulthood can return in an amazing way as wonder and curiosity, adventure and magic possess every fibre of our being. This is a self-discovery – a power that awakens the senses, the spirit and the fire. Without this dynamism and vitality, life can be tedious and shallow, boring and dull. If your heart is empty, the rest really doesn't matter much.

Each of us has a precious gift, a potential, a reason. The true wonder of the world is available everywhere – in the minutest parts of our bodies, in the vast expanses of the cosmos, and in the intimate inter-connectedness of these and all things. We each have so much to give, so many talents. Each of us is so blessed if we could only see it. It's only when we live out, and give, that love which is inside us, that we awaken and become who we are, part of the mystery, part of each other, part of the hymn of the universe. This spiritual journey, indivisible from caring for each other, is the purpose of our lives – to love and celebrate each other as one. The secret is usually hidden only because we stand with our backs to the light while it is shining at us all the time.

Becoming light is not always a deepening of our personal reality nor is it always a pleasant journey. It's certainly little to do with churches and seldom is it an intellectual realisation. Rarely do we notice that we are in the midst of the extraordinary. Miracles occur all around us, signs show us the way, angels plead to be heard, but we pay little attention to them for our culture has conditioned us to think all the time. The Western world has become very distracted from itself. We talk too much and, if we pray, we often use words because we are used to using words to express thoughts. But prayer is a disposition, a state of life, part of everything we do. It is in the very fibre of the simple normal actions. In the Cloud of Unknowing, one of the great mystical texts of the fourteenth century, the author wrote 'this is not attained by study, but by grace. We must pray in the height, depth, length and breadth of the spirit without many words but with a single word.' Unless we take our complete selves, our true selves, into silence, we are pretending. If we make love, we bring our whole energy, body, mind and soul to the beloved and share with them our naked selves. How much more so in prayer as we bring our rage, our doubts, our passions, our vunerabilities before the hidden.

It is also about the rare gift of listening. True listening, no matter how brief, requires tremendous effort. It requires the absolute focusing of the mind, the emptying of oneself and concentrating on the other. It would be wise for us to learn the art of listening. The Maasai are very good listeners. They can really listen in a way that pours the whole of themselves into your presence. Listening is not easy. It takes a lot of emotional resources. In our work with the terminally ill, I have found that those who care for the dying burn out, not from the distress of physically managing the multiple infectious diseases but from the emotional drain of listening.

Throughout history, mystical traditions from the Tao and the Bhagavad Gita to Zen teachings and the early sages, have all tried to express the importance of thinking outside the limitations of the senses, the letting go of our ideas and preconceptions. Let go this 'everywhere' and this 'everything'; exchange it for 'nowhere' and 'nothing'. We should not be worried if we don't understand the idea of the 'nothing'. It is simply the space and silence that allows the spirit to be. At the same time, it is so important that no thinking about it can do it justice anyway.

Once in Ethiopia I was visiting a tiny Coptic monastery and was chatting to one of the monks. He told me that in his view we should let go of thinking and not worry about working things out, and just taste the sense of nothing. The centre, that we all search for, is already inside us. It is not in some remote Buddhist temple or in an ancient scroll. It is here, now, in the ordinary things around us or rather, how we encounter them. We do not need answers, only insight. Knowledge is a very small thing, but what is within your heart is everything. This is what life is for. To awaken ourselves to the stillness within our hearts that is part of the greater stillness of us all.

We are what lives within our hearts.
We are what we give. We are what we
celebrate in the moment of our presence
in this life. Our deeds spring from the love
within. The love in us pours from our
union within. Our union within comes
from being awake. Being awake comes
from inner stillness. Inner stillness comes
from silence. And silence is the door to
compassion, to serenity. To a life of love
and freedom

We need space in our lives to find ourselves, to discover silence and the energy within our hearts. We need time to let go of our thoughts and judgments, fears and chains. We must leap into the unknown and embrace the hidden as we create and wonder and explore. We must ask what we can do? What can we share? How can I celebrate? How can I give?

> 'We who lived in concentration camps
> can remember the men who walked
> through the huts comforting others,
> giving away their last piece of bread.
> They may have been few in number,
> but they offered sufficient proof that
> everything can be taken from a man but
> one thing: the last of human freedoms
> – to choose one's attitude in any given
> set of circumstances, to choose one's own
> way. And there were always choices to
> make. Every day, every hour, offered the
> opportunity to make a decision; a decision
> which determined whether you would or
> would not submit to those powers which
> threatened to rob you of your very self,
> your inner freedom; which determined
> whether or not you would become the
> plaything of circumstance...'
> Victor Frankl

We do not have to be brave; we just have to be half way decent human beings.

The key to everything is patience. We have to re-learn the art of waiting. In the Western world, we have become particularly bad at being patient. We run on moving escalators, we fight and become anxious if we have to wait even a few minutes. We complain when we are delayed. Just think about the times in the last few days when you felt moments of impatience, times when you just wanted to be going faster. We are only passing through so fleetingly. I am often amused by friends, some of whom devote all their energies to collecting things that they are going to leave behind anyway. It's much more fun to share them around. We were meant to really enjoy life, to delight in it, explore it, be fascinated with it, be full of wonder and awe. The moment we lose that delicious thrill and excitement, a flame dies in us. The good news is, of course, that it can be rekindled. It begins with awareness of the mysterious occurrences that can change one's life, the feeling that some other process is operating.

It is a process in which we may make many mistakes but in which there are many victories too. It is my belief that unless I try to help the wounded, the weak, the vulnerable and do so from the most intimate part of me, I am living only a small part of what I could be... If I cry tears of sorrow every day, so too do I laugh and rejoice so much more. Unless I bring into my heart the all of us, the whole of us, my humanity is unfulfilled in my time here. When we do the best that we can, we never know what miracle is wrought in our life, or in the life of another. When we treat man as he is, we make him worse than he is; when we treat him as if he already were what he potentially could be, we make him what he should be.

It is easy to tell people to never be afraid of living your dream and not to settle for less than love. But living dreams is never quite so easy and we don't change lifestyles that have been conditioned by decades of social behaviour and cultural programming overnight. However, we can make sense of our journey, we can cast out our fears and we can realise our full potential. In order to do so we need to radically question the sum total of our existence and whether or not it is enough, or if we should demand more out of life and from the gifts that are within us. In my own journey, every day is ever more amazing to me, filled with ever more possibilities, pleasures and opportunities. I delight in finding new friends, new ways to explore being me, discovering new ways of understanding and perceiving the world as it unfolds, new vistas that open up other horizons. As we create and change and become, we learn how very little we know. Then we realise that knowing is not especially important anyway – what matters is living and caring and loving. The Dalai Lama puts it this way:

'With two hands joined... I appeal to you to make the rest of your life as meaningful as possible.'

Each day we should seek to become, seek to rejoice, to celebrate, to heal, to love, to be ourselves in the richest fullest sense. This means proactively engaging in everything around us. Becoming one with others, with those familiar and unfamiliar, seeing everything in a completely different way, slowly creating new behaviours and habits. Anything less than a conscious commitment to the important is an unconscious commitment to the unimportant. We can begin by giving little gifts of our selves, random acts of hidden kindness and caring, a smile, a blessing, an embrace. We can become more cherishing, more tender, more a bringer of calm and humour and laughter into the ordinariness of our day. This can change everything around us. There is a Samburu saying, 'If you live today and have not laughed, it is a day you have laid in your grave.'

In our worlds, we need to make a determined effort to make more time for those we love, to communicate from our hearts, to create more personal silence and space for ourselves, to look after each other with respect and kindness. We must also seize new opportunities, discover something about ourselves every day, develop a curiosity and grow as people. We must tend our hearts and work at developing our gifts. We have the capacity to engage the world with positive creative love. If we are enjoying life, it will show. If we show people we value them and consider them very special, we will open in them new opportunities to love. At the dawn of this millennium the Dalai Lama wrote:

> *'Treat everyone like a close friend. I say this neither as Dalai Lama nor as someone who has special powers or ability. Of these, I have none. I speak as a human being: one who, like yourselves, wishes to be happy and not to suffer'.*

We have the opportunity to change people's lives every time we meet them – whatever we do there is unlimited potential. The miracle is that the more we share, the more we have or, in the Words of John of the Cross, the only thing we take with us when we die are what we gave away.

My prayer is that one day we will look back with awe and joy at our lives and delight in the grace, wonder and power therein, for it is one and the same journey, yours and mine. In the end it is about discovering the one essential truth that in all things, everything is made whole through love – all suffering, doubt, anxiety and pain is eclipsed. That in all things, all that lasts, all that brings us joy, is love. Born of our inner hearts freely given and shared. He to whom this emotion is a stranger, who can no longer pause to wonder and stand rapt in awe, is as good as dead: his eyes are closed.

I believe that each of us has within him an energy, a thread of life, that is shared by all creation. We have within us a connection, a primal spark. That spark is at the heart of this book. We share the life force and are part of a miracle, part of a promise. In the end words matter very little. I have always believed it is our actions, not our thoughts, that matter. Tears have never fed a child, pity has never healed a wound. Unless words become deeds, unless dreams are lived, they are mere deceptions. Despite our weakness, because of our frailty, we can touch each other with light and change each other with gentleness. We have the power to become light. In a world of brokenness, we can bring wonder. Where there are tears, we can bring laughter. Where there is trembling and loneliness, we can bring love. We were not meant to have compassion, we were meant to become compassionate. With all my heart I believe that this is why we were born.

Epilogue:
The Football Lesson

Shortly after finishing the draft of this book, I was in a small village in the African desert. This village is a dusty, sprawling collection of huts and crumbling structures on the Somali border. I was visiting an old friend who runs a school and medical project there. Jementa has been working in Africa since before I was born. Now there is heat, there is humid heat, then there's equatorial dry heat but this – this was hotter than hell. Jamenta and I went out to the back yard to sit on the veranda. We talked mostly about skiing and truck repairs for she is a true Austrian nurse with a passion for all things mechanical.

It was late afternoon when I heard the children playing. Leaving Jamenta to work, I strolled over, between the palms, to watch the kids' football match. Their laughter guided me to them; that and the dust cloud that surrounded their play. It was only then that I realised why there was so much dust. There they were, some thirty kids playing, chasing after the ball, calling out, giggling, laughing – only, they were not complete. Some were without arms, others without legs, most were landmine victims from the Somali war. The few children who did have feet were scrambling around with the others, oblivious to their team-mates' disabilities. The kids didn't even really have a ball; just a homemade effort tied up with string. I spoke to one girl who had no hands and she explained to me where the imaginary lines were, then giggled. I stepped back quickly, I was on the pitch!

One boy, Ali, arrived in a cloud of dust right beside me, he was about 14. The ball had gone up the pitch, followed by the same calls and intensity found in any serious match. Ali smiled at me, his eyes darting to the field of play, then smiling back at me. His legs had been blown off below the knees. He told me what number he was playing and who his favourite players in the English League were – I agreed enthusiastically, knowing nothing about soccer. Then I asked him if it was harder to play football now than before. Ali was poised to charge up the wing but he smiled and said *"haua utagi kuwana megu kuchesa impia"*, then vanished down the line heading the ball. And that's the truth. You don't need feet to play football.

Just like Ali, we too have a choice. We can love or we can hate. We can break the moulds set by others or remain trapped inside them. We can decide to give, not take. We can decide not to be overcome, not to be helpless. Happiness is letting go of self-preoccupation and celebrating all the possibilities that are around you now. It's how you close this book and look at your own power, your own horizons. This freedom transforms everything forever. When I play on the field of life knowing this in my heart, I truly know that all will be well.

ICROSS

ICROSS is a small grassroots NGO active in Kenya and Tanzania. It was founded in 1981 and now has 18-years experience of effectively implementing a wide-range of community-based health care.

Mission Statement:

To reduce disease, suffering and poverty among the most deprived communities through development projects run by the people themselves, using their language and their belief and value systems.

Aims of ICROSS

- To prevent disease and reduce morbidity
- To provide low cost, high quality preventative and curative health services where needed
- To provide home-based care at home for the terminally ill (particularly AIDS patients)
- To improve mother and child health
- To support the development of women's organisations in rural populations
- To assist marginalised communities to protect their legal rights and entitlements
- To demonstrate outcomes of development through action research
- To use and disseminate findings of research and lessons learned both locally and internationally
- To create a new awareness and a sense of equality and unity between the rich and poor worlds

www.icross.ie

www.icross-international.net

About Eye Books

Eye books is a young, dynamic publishing company that likes to break the rules. Our independence allows us to publish books which challenge the way people see things. It also means that we can offer new authors a platform from which they can shine their light and encourage others to do the same.

To date we have published 35 books that cover a number of genres including Travel, Biography, Adventure and History. Many of our books are experience driven. All of them are inspirational and life-affirming.

Frigid Women, for example, tells the story of the world-record making first all female expedition to the North Pole. A fifty year-old mother of three who had recently recovered from a mastectomy, and her daughter are the authors neither had ever written a book before. Sue Riches is now both author and highly sought after motivational speaker.

We also publish thematic anthologies, such as The Tales from Heaven and Hell series, for those who prefer the short story format. Here everyone has the chance to get their stories published and win prizes such as flights to any destination in the world.

And here's what makes us really different: As well as publishing books, Eye Books has set up a club for like-minded people and is in the process of developing a number of initiatives and services for its community of members. After all, the more you put into life, the more you get out of it.

Please visit www.eye-books.com for further information.

Eye Club Membership

Each month, we receive hundreds of enquiries' from people who have read our books, discovered our website or entered our competitions. All of these people have certain things in common; a desire to achieve, to extend the boundaries of everyday life and to learn from others' experiences.

Eye Books has, therefore, set up a club to unite these like-minded people. It is a community where members can exchange ideas, contact authors, discuss travel, both future and past as well as receive information and offers from ourselves.

Membership is free.

Benefits of the Eye Club

As a member of the Eye Club:

• You are offered the invaluable opportunity to contact our authors directly.
• You will be able to receive a regular newsletter, information on new book releases and company developments as well as discounts on new and past titles.
• You can attend special member events such as book launches, author talks and signings.
• Receive discounts on a variety of travel related products and services from Eye Books partners.
• In addition, you can enjoy entry into Eye Books competitions including the ever popular Heaven and Hell series and our monthly book competition.

To register your membership, simply visit our website and register on our club pages: www.eye-books.com.

New Titles

Riding the Outlaw Trail - Simon Casson
A true story of an epic horseback journey by two Englishmen from Mexico to Canada, across 2,000 miles of some of America's most difficult terrain. Their objective? To retrace the footsteps of those legendary real life bandits Butch Cassidy and the Sundance Kid, by riding the outlaw trails they rode more than a century ago.
ISBN: 1 903070 228. Price £9.99.

Desert Governess - Phyllis Ellis
Phyllis, a former Benny Hill actress, takes on a new challenge when she becomes a governess to the Saudi Arabian Royal family. In this frank personal memoir, she gives us an insider's view into the Royal family and a woman's role in this mysterious kingdom.
ISBN: 1 903070 015. Price £9.99.

Last of the Nomads - W. J. Peasley
Warri and Yatungka were the last of the desert nomads to live permanently in the traditional way. Their deaths marked the end of a tribal lifestyle that stretched back more than 30,000 years. The Last of the Nomads tells of an extraordinary journey in search of Warri and Yatungka, their rescue and how they survived alone for thirty years in the unrelenting Western Desert region of Australia.
ISBN: 1 903070 325. Price £9.99.

First Contact - Mark Anstice
This is a true story of a modern day exploration by two young adventurers and the discovery of cannibal tribes in the 21st century. An expedition far more extraordinary than they had ever imagined, one that would stretch them, their friendship and their equipment to the limits.
ISBN: 1 903070 260. Price £9.99.

Further Travellers' Tales From Heaven and Hell - Various
This is the third book in the series, after the first two best selling
Travellers' Tales from Heaven and Hell. It is an eclectic collection
of over a hundred anecdotal travel stories which will enchant you,
shock you and leave you in fits of laughter!
ISBN: 1 903070 112. Price £9.99.

Special Offa - Bob Bibby
Following his last best selling book Dancing with Sabrina, Bob
walks the length of Offa's Dyke. He takes us through the towns
and villages that have sprung up close by and reveals their
ancient secrets and folklore. He samples the modern day with his
refreshingly simple needs and throws light on where to go and
what to see.
ISBN: 1 903070 287. Price £9.99.

The Good Life - Dorian Amos
Needing a change and some adventure, Dorian and his wife
searched their world atlas and decided to sell up and move to
Canada. Having bought Pricey the car, Boris Lock their faithful dog,
a canoe and their fishing equipment they set off into the Yukon
Wilderness to find a place they could call home.
ISBN: 1 903070 309. Price £9.99.

Baghdad Business School - Heyrick Bond Gunning
A camp bed, ten cans of baked beans, some water and $25,000
is all that was needed to set up an International Business in Iraq.
The book chronicles an amusing description of the trials and
tribulations of doing business in an environment where explosions
and shootings are part of everyday life, giving the reader a unique
insight into what is really happening in this country.
ISBN: 1 903070 333. Price £9.99.

Green Oranges on Lion Mountain - Emily Joy
Armed with a beginner's guide to surgery, GP Emily Joy took up
her VSO posting at a remote hospital in Sierra Leone. As she set off
into the unknown, action, adventure and romance were high on
her agenda; rebel forces and the threat of civil war were not.
ISBN: 1 903070 295. Price £9.99.

The Con Artists Handbook - Joel Levy
Get wise with The Con Artist's Handbook as it blows the lid on the
secrets of the successful con artist and his con games. Get inside
the hustler's head and find out what makes him tick; Learn how the
world's most infamous scams are set up and performed; Peruse the
career profiles of the most notorious scammers and hustlers of all time;
Learn to avoid the modern-day cons of the e-mail and Internet age.
ISBN: 1 903070 341. Price £9.99.

The Forensics Handbook - Pete Moore
The Forensic Handbook is the most up-to-date log of forensic techniques available. Discover how the crime scene is examined using
examples of some of the most baffling crimes; Learn techniques of
lifting, comparing and identifying prints; Calculate how to examine
blood splatter patterns; Know what to look for when examining
explosive deposits, especially when terrorist activity is suspected.
Learn how the Internet is used to trace stalkers.
ISBN: 1 903070 35X. Price £9.99.

Also by Eye Books

Jasmine and Arnica - Nicola Naylor
A blind woman's journey around India.
ISBN: 1 903070 171. Price £9.99.

Touching Tibet - Niema Ash
A journey into the heart of this intriguing forbidden kingdom.
ISBN: 1 903070 18X. Price £9.99.

Behind the Veil - Lydia Laube
A shocking account of a nurses Arabian nightmare.
ISBN: 1 903070 198. Price £9.99.

Walking Away - Charlotte Metcalf
A well known film makers African journal.
ISBN: 1 903070 201. Price £9.99.

Travels in Outback Australia - Andrew Stevenson
In search of the original Australians - the Aboriginal People.
ISBN: 1 903070 147. Price £9.99

The European Job - Jonathan Booth
10,000 miles around Europe in a 25 year old classic car.
ISBN: 1 903070 252. Price £9.99

Around the World with 1000 Birds - Russell Boyman
An extraordinary answer to a mid-life crisis.
ISBN: 1 903070 163. Price £9.99

Cry from the Highest Mountain - Tess Burrows
A climb to the point furthest from the centre of the earth.
ISBN: 1 903070 120. Price £9.99

Dancing with Sabrina - Bob Bibby
A journey from source to sea of the River Severn.
ISBN: 1 903070 244. Price £9.99

Grey Paes and Bacon - Bob Bibby
A journey around the canals of the Black Country
ISBN: 1 903070 066. Price £7.99

Jungle Janes - Peter Burden
Twelve middle-aged women take on the Jungle. As seen on Ch 4.
ISBN: 1 903070 05 8. Price £7.99

Travels with my Daughter - Niema Ash
Forget convention, follow your instincts.
ISBN: 1 903070 04 X. Price £7.99

Riding with Ghosts - Gwen Maka
One woman's solo cycle ride from Seattle to Mexico.
ISBN: 1 903070 00 7. Price £7.99

Riding with Ghosts: South of the Border - Gwen Maka
The second part of Gwen's epic cycle trip across the Americas.
ISBN: 1 903070 09 0. Price £7.99

Triumph Round the World - Robbie Marshall
He gave up his world for the freedom of the road.
ISBN: 1 903070 08 2. Price £7.99

Fever Trees of Borneo - Mark Eveleigh
A daring expedition through uncharted jungle.
ISBN: 0 953057 56 9. Price £7.99

Discovery Road - Tim Garrett and Andy Brown
Their mission was to mountain bike around the world.
ISBN: 0 953057 53 4. Price £7.99

Frigid Women - Sue and Victoria Riches
The first all-female expedition to the North Pole.
ISBN: 0 953057 52 6. Price £7.99

Jungle Beat - Roy Follows
Fighting Terrorists in Malaya.
ISBN: 0 953057 57 7. Price £7.99

Slow Winter - Alex Hickman
A personal quest against the backdrop of the war-torn Balkans.
ISBN: 0 953057 58 5. Price £7.99

Tea for Two - Polly Benge
She cycled around India to test her love.
ISBN: 0 953057 59 3. Price £7.99

Traveller's Tales from Heaven and Hell - Various
A collection of short stories from a nationwide competition.
ISBN: 0 953057 51 8. Price £6.99

More Traveller's Tales from Heaven and Hell - Various
The second collection of short stories.
ISBN: 1 903070 02 3. Price £6.99

A Trail of Visions: Route 1 - Vicki Couchman
A stunning photographic essay.
ISBN: 1 871349 338. Price £14.99

A Trail of Visions: Route 2 - Vicki Couchman
The second stunning photographic essay.
ISBN: 0 953057 50 X. Price £16.99

Book Microsites

If you are interested in finding out more about our books, we have created microsites for a number of our titles including:

First Contact
Riding The Outlaw Trail
Desert Governess
The Last of the Nomads
Special Offa
The Good Life
Green Oranges on Lion Mountain
Baghdad Business School

For details on these sites and others which we are developing please visit our main website:

www.eye-books.com

Special Offers and Promotions

We are offering our club members and people who have read this book the opportunity to take advantage of promotions on our other books by buying direct from us.

For information on these special offers please visit the following page of our website:

www.eye-books.com/promotions.htm